Genesis Unbound is a startlingly refreshing and innovativ~
the text of Genesis 1–2. It is an altogether n~
needed rapprochement between the
Not everyone will adopt all of the feat\
text, but all will find plenty to challen\
might have previously thought were con   .. ɪnis
volume will be talked about for years to c\

WALTER C. KAISE   ,.\..

Colman M. Mockler Distinguished Professor of Old Testament
Gordon-Conwell Theological Seminary

In many ways traditional or classical in his approach, Sailhamer is at the
same time innovative and creative (no pun intended). He will force you to
rethink your current understanding of the Genesis creation narrative.

RONALD YOUNGBLOOD

Professor of Old Testament and Hebrew
Bethel Theological Seminary

If you think you know what Genesis 1 and 2 say, you may, after reading
Genesis Unbound be not a little surprised at what you have missed.
Sailhamer, anything but conventional, strips away interpretive barnacles
in this careful and stimulating analysis. He is in touch with current scholarship, but he significantly capitalizes on input by commentators from an
earlier, pre-scientific period. In *Genesis Unbound* he proposes that all but
the first verse of Genesis 1 and 2 have to do with God preparing the land
of Palestine for Israel. Sound far-fetched? Follow the clues in the text and
Sailhamer's arguments. Compelling? More so than one might first think.
This is a work by an author unbound except for being intent on listening
to the biblical text. Sailhamer has so focused on the text itself that his work
must be taken seriously. Here is a refreshing visit to a fundamental scripture by an evangelical scholar of stature.

ELMER A. MARTENS, PH.D.

Professor Emeritus of OT
Mennonite Brethren Biblical Seminary

Many book titles promise more than they can deliver. *Genesis Unbound*, however, yields more than first meets the eye. Not only is the reader furnished a provocative new interpretation of Genesis 1 and 2, but he is treated to a lesson in hermeneutical exercise. Professor Sailhamer invites us to think carefully through these creation accounts in the full light of their grammatical, historical and cultural, literary, and theological contexts so that through the text we may understand what the original author intended his readers to know. All of this is presented in a lucid and lively style that is sure to stimulate today's readers to examine their own previous approaches to these crucial chapters.

RICHARD PATTERSON
Professor Emeritus, Liberty University

Genesis Unbound represents a fresh and provocative challenge to traditional, classical, and popular understanding of the first two chapters of the Bible by one of today's foremost evangelical authorities on the Book of Genesis. Dr. Sailhamer's conclusions are based upon a detailed analysis of the biblical text and a thorough understanding of the history of its interpretation. But the structure and style of presentation are deliberately geared to lay readers. All who wrestle with the perplexing questions raised by the biblical account of creation will welcome this study by a scholar with an uncompromisingly high view of Scripture.

DANIEL L. BLOCK, PH.D.
Professor of Old Testament Interpretation
The Southern Baptist Theological Seminary

Genesis Unbound is a truly unique book. The book presents a fresh, yet apparently ancient perspective on the early chapters of Genesis. This book needs to be read, pondered, and perhaps read again by all who seek to understand these crucial early chapters of Genesis.

RAYMOND G. BOHLIN, PH.D.
Director of Research, Probe Ministries

Always provocative, John Sailhamer once again rattles traditional preconceptions about an important biblical text. Well researched and creative, *Genesis Unbound* re-presents a medieval Jewish view of the creation account and suggests that this reading helps resolve the age-old debate between science and religion. Even if one doesn't accept his final conclusions, John Sailhamer challenges and unsettles the inappropriate smugness that characterizes much evangelical exposition of Genesis 1 and 2.

TREMPER LONGMAN III
Westminster Theological Seminary

GENESIS UNBOUND

A PROVOCATIVE NEW LOOK AT THE CREATION ACCOUNT

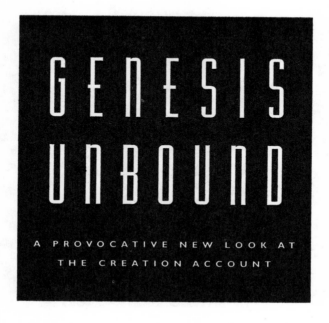

GENESIS UNBOUND

A PROVOCATIVE NEW LOOK AT
THE CREATION ACCOUNT

DR. JOHN H. SAILHAMER

MULTNOMAH BOOKS • SISTERS, OREGON

GENESIS UNBOUND
published by Multnomah Books
a part of the Questar publishing family

© 1996 by John H. Sailhamer

International Standard Book Number: 0-88070-868-9

Cover illustration by Tom Collicott
Cover design by David Uttley

Printed in the United States of America

For information:
QUESTAR PUBLISHERS, INC.
POST OFFICE BOX 1720
SISTERS, OREGON 97759

96 97 98 99 00 01 02 03 — 10 9 8 7 6 5 4 3 2 1

CONTENTS

PREFACE

What does the title *Genesis Unbound* mean? Is the first book in the Bible "bound" in some way? Does it need to be "unbound"? If it does, am I the one to do it?

Let me explain what I mean by that title. I believe we often read the first two chapters of Genesis with a set of unexamined assumptions. We come to these chapters with certain expectations and are surprised when difficulties in understanding the passage arise.

What are those expectations? One is that the chapters' primary purpose is merely to describe how God created the world. Another is that originally the world was a formless mass, which God shaped into the world we know today. A third is "the land" which God made during the six days is "the earth" in its entirety, as we know it today. Those assumptions, and others, largely guide our reading of this important passage of Scripture.

How do I know that? I know it because those assumptions lie behind the English translations of Genesis 1 and 2 which we use today. Like it or not, Genesis in the English Bible is "bound" by those assumptions. A major part of my task in this book is to loose those bonds and release the chapters to speak for themselves. Hence, the title.

Who am I to take on such a formidable group of scholars as the translators of our English Bibles? Believe me, I am not worthy of the task. That is why as you read you will see I make much use of the work of others, particularly the wealth of biblical scholarship from the past. In the modern era, readers of the Bible have tried to harmonize Genesis 1 and 2 with the dictates of modern science. That, of course, is a legitimate goal, but it has its downside. Too often we allow our modern views of the world to determine what we understand the biblical writers to be saying. By paying close attention to how earlier readers understood these two chapters, we can often gain new insight — or old insight — into the biblical author's intent.

So although several points I make in this book may strike you as new, many of them are, in fact, quite old.

You will soon see that I have included drawings throughout the book. By providing these drawings, I don't mean to imply that my readers aren't capable of visualizing what I am writing about. I have found, however, after years of teaching this material, that subtle nuances are often misunderstood without the sketches to illustrate the points. So the drawings are here to help prevent that kind of misunderstanding.

Finally, I wish to thank several persons for the help they have given me in preparing and writing this book. I want to thank, first, the staff at Questar Publishers, including the primary editor for this work, Steve Halliday. If this book makes sense, it is because of Steve's and others' indefatigable labors to make it so. I would also like to thank the many students with whom I have studied Genesis over the years. Their questions and observations have continually caused me to go back to the text for answers about its meaning. Some of my best students were found in my adult Sunday school class at the North Suburban Evangelical Free Church in Deerfield, Illinois. They patiently and faithfully listened, literally for years, as I painstakingly worked my way through the early chapters of Genesis with them Sunday after Sunday.

As always, I owe the most to my good friend and wife, Patty.

A CARD SHARK I'M NOT

Although I'm not much of a card player, even I understand that in most games it's best to conceal your hand until the end. Revealing your cards only ensures a losing streak. The whole idea is to take your opponents by surprise.

I'm not a novelist either, but I've read enough good stories to know that accomplished authors normally save their best stuff for last. They weave a tale of intrigue and suspense and heart-racing action until, on the last page, they unveil a startling twist.

You're about to discover why I'm neither a card shark nor a successful novelist. You see, right at the beginning I want to show you my hand and reveal some of my best plot twists. I want you to know what's ahead; only then will I back up and build my case for why you should believe me. It may seem a little backwards, but you'll see why I chose this route in a little bit.

A QUICK OVERVIEW

Genesis Unbound will argue that a common modern understanding of the first two chapters of Genesis is simply wrong. Because of this error, many Christians have felt torn between an allegiance to the Bible and a recognition of the findings of modern science — a tear that is neither necessary nor helpful.

One of the main purposes for this book is to show that when Genesis 1 and 2 are understood as I believe Moses intended them to be understood, nearly all of the difficulties that perplex modern readers instantly vanish. Through a fresh reading of Genesis 1:1–2:4a that builds on the work of gifted interpreters from centuries past — an approach I call "Historical Creationism" — I try to show how this can be so. My approach is textual and biblical, not primarily scientific or historical. I come to the text as an evangelical Christian committed to the inerrancy of the Scriptures and as one who wants to hear what the Bible itself means to say.

I maintain that the narratives of Genesis 1 and 2 are to be understood as both literal and historical. They recount two great acts of God. In the first act, God created the universe we see around us today, consisting of the earth, the sun, the moon, the stars, and all the plants and animals that now inhabit (or formerly inhabited) the earth. The biblical record of that act of creation is recounted in Genesis 1:1 — "In the beginning, God created the heavens and the earth."

Since the Hebrew word translated "beginning" refers to an indefinite period of time, we cannot say for certain when God created the world or how long He took to create it. This period could have spanned as much as several billion years, or it could have been much less; the text simply does not tell us how long. It tells us only that God did it during the "beginning" of our universe's history.

The second act of God recounted in Genesis 1 and 2 deals with a much more limited scope and period of time. Beginning with Genesis 1:2, the biblical narrative recounts God's preparation of a land for the man and woman He was to create. That "land" was the same land later promised to Abraham and his descendants. It was that land which God gave to Israel after their exodus from Egypt. It was that land to which Joshua led the Israelites after their time of wandering in the wilderness. According to Genesis 1, God prepared that land within a period of a six-day work week. On the sixth day of that week, God created human beings. God then rested on the seventh day.

The second chapter of Genesis provides a closer look at God's creation of the first human beings. We are told that God created them from the ground and put them in the garden of Eden to worship and obey God (not merely to work the garden and take care of it). The boundaries of that garden are the same as those of the promised land; thus the events of these chapters foreshadow the events of the remainder of the Pentateuch. God creates a people, He puts them into the land He has prepared for them, and He calls on them to worship and obey Him and receive His blessing.

WHAT'S AHEAD?

With that conceptual overview in mind, now allow me to present in brief the major sections of this book. As we progress, we'll unpack each feature one by one, then put them all together. By the time we're finished, if I've done what a good teacher is supposed to do, the light should go on for you.

In Part One we'll see why this issue is so important. It's been my experience that untold thousands of Christians struggle to maintain a biblical faith in our modern, scientific age. They're almost embarrassed by Genesis 1 and 2. These first chapters seem so archaic, so outdated, so *ancient*. How could anyone take them seriously?

I insist that not only can we take seriously these first two chapters of the Bible, but they fit in remarkably well with our current scientific models of the universe. And they do so on their own terms, *without* forcing the reader to do somersaults in logic or to inject foreign ideas into the text.

In Part Two I roll out the biggest guns in my arsenal. In many ways this section is the heart of the book. Several weighty pieces of evidence will be marshaled to construct a coherent and, I hope, accurate picture of what Moses intended to say to us in Genesis 1 and 2. What you'll find here may surprise you — and some of it may cause you to squirm a bit. Why? Because these critical pieces of evidence challenge a commonly accepted view...a view that you may hold at this very moment! Yet I'm convinced that the arguments I cite in Part Two not only point the way to a proper understanding of the first two chapters of Genesis, but they also enable us to live in peace with the findings of modern science.

In Part Three we'll walk through a brief exposition of Genesis 1:1–2:4a, building on the foundations laid previously in the book. If you're the kind of reader who likes to read the last chapter of a mystery first, you might want to start *Genesis Unbound* by reading this section. After you know how the "mystery" ends, you could backtrack to earlier sections to see how I reached my conclusions.

Part Four is designed for those who want to go a bit deeper into the issues, for those who want to get a better sense of the historical, philosophical, and interpretive issues that brought us to where we are today. In this part I explain where some common — but I think erroneous — interpretations of Genesis came from. Is it possible that a few archaic notions, which no one takes seriously today, still exert enormous influence on the way we view Genesis? I think that's exactly what has happened, and in Part Four I show you how this came to be.

However you approach the book, my great hope is that you will come away with a new appreciation for and understanding of the genius of these first two chapters of the Bible. We should be awed and grateful that God chose to give us this remarkable peek into His mighty works at the dawn of time!

A FINAL WORD

One last word. Even among those who take Genesis 1 as God's Word and as a true statement of the facts, there remain significant differences of opinion about what the text actually says. We must never forget that good and godly people can find themselves on opposite sides of basic questions about these chapters.

Although we will focus almost entirely on Genesis 1 and 2, we would do well to begin our investigation by recalling the words of the Apostle Paul, written centuries after the time of Moses: "If I have the gift of prophecy and can fathom all mysteries and all knowledge, and if I have a faith that can move mountains, but have not love, I am nothing" (1 Corinthians 13:2).

My intention in *Genesis Unbound* is not to tweak other evangelical noses, nor is it to condemn or unfairly portray those with whom I disagree. It does no good to be right if your spirit is wrong. My hope is that this book will shed helpful light on a very old and very difficult problem. If the views presented here accurately reflect what the author of Genesis 1 and 2 had in mind when he wrote his own book so long ago, then I pray that God would use them to magnify His Word and make it plain. If I am mistaken, however, then I pray that my well-intentioned views would do no great harm and that they would slip into a quickly forgotten past.

In such a spirit of congenial discovery I now invite you to join me as we look carefully at the crucial words of Genesis 1 and 2.

PART ONE

GENESIS IN CONTROVERSY

• Although the first two chapters of Genesis present difficult problems of interpretation, we must remember that they were written to be understood. Our task is to read them as the author intended them to be understood.

• The primary question for any interpreter must always be, What does the text say? Science and history may provide interesting and helpful insights, but the focus of all interpretation must be on the text itself.

• Just because an interpretation is commonly held doesn't mean it's correct.

CHAPTER ONE

WHAT'S ALL THE FUSS?

ew passages in Scripture have prompted so many different inter-pretations as have the first two chapters of Genesis. Virtually every word and certainly every verse has been combed, poked, and pulled apart in search of clues to solve the mystery of crea-tion. The territory has been well charted. Claims have been staked. Battles have raged over the many lines drawn in the textual sands of these early chapters of Genesis.

Martin Luther once said of Genesis 1 that "it contains things the most important, and at the same time the most obscure."[1] Luther himself despaired of ever truly understanding the meaning of this chapter. There was none before him, said the great Reformer, "who could explain all these momentous things, with sufficient appropriateness and success: For inter-preters and commentators have confused and entangled them with such a variety, diversity, and infinity of questions, that it is sufficiently plain, that God has reserved the majesty of this wisdom, and the full and sound understanding of this chapter, to himself alone."[2] About the only thing we can be sure of in this chapter, Luther concluded, was "that the world began, and was made of God, out of nothing."[3]

Had Luther lived longer, he would have learned that even these two points would eventually be called into question!

Along with Luther we may easily despair over the seeming impossi-bility of making sense out of this text. And yet it was written to be under-stood. Luther himself recognized this. Even after expressing his doubts about understanding the first chapter of Genesis, Luther wrote an extensive commentary on it. His insights into the meaning of Genesis 1 mark one of the most important stages in the long history of its interpretation. Although Luther himself stood in the stream of biblical interpretation, he managed to change the course of the river. Nowhere is that more true than in Genesis 1 and 2.

Although Luther was right — a vast range of questions do confront us in Genesis 1 — the text itself offers clues that promise to throw open the shades and let the light of biblical truth shine in. I believe we may come to a proper understanding of Genesis 1 and 2.

BUT IT'S SO CLEAR!

Despite Luther's position, many people believe the meaning of Genesis 1 and 2 is clear and that the only real issue is whether they are true. In teaching I have often found myself with two students in the same classroom who expressed radically different views about the meaning of Genesis 1, yet each one assumed he or she held the commonly accepted point of view. Many of these students who believe they hold a "traditional" understanding of Genesis 1 are surprised to discover that they actually espouse a very modern, "nontraditional" view.

That is why we shouldn't assume that current conservative or evangelical views of Genesis 1 automatically represent the "traditional" view. More often than not, current assumptions about this chapter are a far cry from traditional views.

For example, one widely held, contemporary, evangelical view of Genesis 1 takes the first verse to be a title for the rest of the chapter.[4] This view says that the words "In the beginning God created the heavens and earth" are not meant to describe a particular act of God but to identify what God did during the week recorded in the remainder of the chapter. Throughout the first chapter God is "creating the heavens and the earth." Therefore, the creation account actually begins in Genesis 1:2 with "And the earth was formless and void...."

What many people fail to realize is that such an understanding of Genesis 1:1 rules out a fundamental notion in the traditional view — the idea that God created the world "out of nothing."[5] If Genesis 1:1 merely summarizes the whole of Genesis 1, then God's acts of creation actually begin in Genesis 1:2. Since the earth was already "formless and void" (vs. 2), that means the earth already existed when God began to act. But if that is so, when did God create the earth?

If Genesis 1:1 is merely a title for the rest of the chapter, then we are left with the uncomfortable discovery that the passage does not tell us when, or who, created the earth. If Genesis 1:1 is merely a title, then Genesis 1 does not teach the traditional concept of "creation out of nothing." That does not invalidate the idea that God created the world "out of nothing" (as Hebrews 11:3 clearly teaches), but it would mean that the notion of "creation out of nothing" is nowhere taught in Genesis 1.

Thus the interpretation that Genesis 1:1 is a title for the chapter — though widely held by modern evangelicals — is anything but traditional. The point, of course, is that we may be surprised to find that our own understandings of Genesis 1 and 2 may not be nearly as "obvious" as we had always thought.

THREE MAJOR VIEWS, YEA THERE ARE FOUR

Evangelicals have typically taken one of three positions when confronted with the possibility of conflict between the Bible and science in the early chapters of Genesis, according to J. P. Moreland.[1]

Those three views are

1. Creationism
2. Progressive Creationism
3. Theistic Evolution
4. Historical Creationism, the viewpoint expressed in this book, is sufficiently different from the other three major views that it warrants being considered as a category of its own. (See page 44 for an explanation of Historical Creationism.)

Each of these major views is profiled in a separate sidebar in this book.

Because the first two chapters of Genesis are among the most familiar portions of the Bible, we can easily take for granted that we understand them. For most of us, they form a basic part of our understanding of the whole of the Bible. We listen to their familiar cadences in much the same way we do the words of the "Star-Spangled Banner" at a ball game or the Pledge of Allegiance in school. We believe the words — or at least we feel we should believe them — but rarely do we read them carefully enough to understand what they really mean. Curiously enough, although Genesis 1 and 2 are among the best known chapters in the Bible, they may also be among the most misunderstood.

My desire in this book is to make clear what I am convinced is the central message of the first two chapters of Genesis. A large part of that task will be dealing with well-worn opinions about these chapters. In many cases those opinions are correct and must be incorporated into a proper interpretation; in other cases they are not correct and need to be replaced with a new understanding.

Throughout church history many people have attempted to explain Genesis 1 and 2 through complicated and mysterious spiritual interpretations. In fact, for many centuries the "spiritual" meaning of Genesis 1 was all the interpreters cared about. Tomes have been written on the spiritual lessons and mysteries of the faith supposedly contained in these early chapters.

I don't intend to add to or focus on such treatments of the text. My concern in *Genesis Unbound* is solely with the meaning of these chapters as intended by their historical author, Moses, who was moved by the Holy Spirit to write the text just as we have it today in the Bible. These texts are inspired by God and represent what He intended to say to us. The meaning is the same for us as it was for the original author. My focus, therefore, will be on the text itself. What do the Hebrew words mean? And what sense does the passage have within the context of the entire book, within the Pentateuch?

Though it is easy to miss, we all are constantly influenced by the world around us when we read Scripture. That influence, whether negative or positive, will always accompany our reading of the text.

Part of the humility required of us as sensitive readers of the Bible is a willingness to seriously look at ourselves as we read. We must listen carefully to the perspective of Scripture, trying hard to distinguish between what we see in the text and what is actually there. Failure to do so can lead to serious error.

An episode from history illustrates what I mean. For many years after the invention of the telescope, scientists believed they saw "canals" on Mars. The idea that intelligent life existed on Mars thus became a common feature of the early "modern" view of the solar system.

After more careful attention was given to the role of the scientists looking through the telescopes, we learned Mars had no "canals." The scientists had seen something real on Mars, but it turned out to be geological formations that merely resembled canals on earth. The "canals" existed only on the small end of the telescope — in the minds of the scientists viewing the distant planet. The data seen through the telescope didn't change over the years; what changed was the interpretation of the data.

A similar problem accompanies all serious reading of Scripture. We can't help trying to make Scripture a part of our world. As long as we live and see our lives from the point of view of our own planet, we will go on viewing the world from that perspective.

If we try, however, we can develop the skill of reading the Bible sensitively and with a willingness to let it change our view of things. Nowhere is this more important than in the study of Genesis 1 and 2.

In the following pages we will take a close look at what is said in the first two chapters of Genesis. We will put them under the microscope, so to speak. And what will we find there? I suspect we may be in for a few surprises.

• It is important to have an informed view of the sense of Genesis 1 and 2 before attempting to relate it to modern scientific viewpoints.

• The view presented in *Genesis Unbound* helps us to better answer the central questions raised by the intersection of Genesis 1 and modern science: the age of the universe, the origin of life, and the validity of the theory of evolution.

CHAPTER TWO

WHAT DIFFERENCE DOES IT MAKE?

or the past two hundred years the understanding of the biblical creation account has gradually shifted. As modern scientific views of the origin of the universe have radically changed, interpretations of the Genesis creation account have been shaped to fit them. Whether we like it or not, modern science has fundamentally altered how we read and understand the Genesis creation account.

The overriding purpose of most recent interpretations of Genesis 1 has been to reconcile these ancient texts with the discoveries of modern science. In many ways, such a concern has always been an important part of biblical apologetics. Each generation must ask how the Bible fits into its world. Yet if we are to understand Genesis 1 correctly, we must first read it on its own terms — *without* attempting to reconcile it with current scientific views. The full, rich, theological message of Genesis 1 and 2 must not be lost in an attempt to harmonize them with modern science. When we know what the biblical view *is*, only then can we attempt to correlate it with science.

My own interpretation of Genesis 1 and 2 has much in common with views developed before the rise of modern science in the late eighteenth and early nineteenth centuries. My view, which I have dubbed Historical Creationism,[1] may appear new and strange to many readers, but it isn't as novel as they might think. In fact, very little of the once-traditional view of

Genesis 1 has survived the onslaught of modern science. More than one modern commentary on Genesis has forced the biblical text through the grid of modern science, in the process leaving in the dust many sound features of the earlier interpretations.

I am convinced that once we understand the original author's perspective in Genesis 1, we will discover that little in this chapter truly conflicts with modern science. Genesis 1 (as well as biblical narratives in general) was intended as a *serious* and *realistic* account of God's work of creation. The creation account is not merely an interesting story; it is written as history.[2]

The goal of this book is to understand the meaning of Genesis 1 and 2 as its original author intended it. Any such view should be evaluated on its own merits. Does it adequately explain the meaning of the text? As Martin Luther noted almost five centuries ago, all interpretations of Genesis 1 and 2 have problems. Yet I contend that the interpretation offered in this book explains more of these difficulties and creates fewer new ones than any other option.

SIX KEY QUESTIONS

At the beginning of our investigation, let's consider six important questions — questions about issues that have frustrated (unnecessarily!) evangelicals for a long time.

1. What does Genesis Unbound *suggest about the age of the universe?*

One of the critical questions we will consider is, What does the Hebrew term "beginning" mean as it is used in Genesis 1:1? The answer to that question has a direct bearing on what we are to believe about the age of the universe. If my interpretation of this term is correct (see chapter 3), then God's creation of the universe *could* have occurred over a vast period of time (although it certainly is not required). In fact, there is no way to limit the duration of the word "beginning" (Hebrew, *reshit*). It could refer to billions of years, to a few thousand years, or to a period as brief as a few months or days. The length of time of this "beginning" is precisely what is left unspecified by the term. The whole point of using *reshit* to convey the concept of "beginning" (when other terms were readily available) is to leave the duration of time unspecified.

Such an understanding of Genesis 1 fits well with most contemporary scientific views of the age of the universe. There is no textual reason why "the beginning" in Genesis 1:1 could not have lasted millions, or even billions, of years. However, the word does not *require* vast time periods; it leaves the duration an open question.

I contend that two distinct time periods are mentioned in Genesis 1. In the first period (the "beginning," Genesis 1:1), God created the universe; no time limitations are placed on that period. In the second period (Genesis 1:2–2:4a), God prepared the garden of Eden for man's dwelling; that activity occurred in one week.

2. What does this interpretation suggest about the supposed long periods of growth and development in the history of the universe, particularly the geological time periods on earth?

I do not speculate on the process by which God created the universe during the "beginning." The Bible does not explain that process. If billions of years really are covered by the simple statement, "In the beginning God created the heavens and the earth," then much of the processes described by modern scientists fall into the period covered by the Hebrew term "beginning." Within that "beginning" would fit the countless geological ages, ice ages, and the many climatic changes on our planet.

The many biological eras would also fit within "the beginning" of Genesis 1:1, including the long ages during which the dinosaurs roamed the earth. By the time human beings were created on the sixth day of the week, the dinosaurs already could have flourished and become extinct — all during the "beginning" recorded in Genesis 1:1.

On the other hand, modern atheistic theories of the origin of the universe certainly are *not* compatible with the statement in Genesis 1:1. The central point of Genesis 1:1 is that *God* created all things. In fact, the biblical creation account can be viewed as a sort of early polemic against atheism.

Genesis 1:1 makes it clear that the world is not eternal; the universe did not create itself. The world had a beginning and it had a Creator. That Creator is the biblical God of the Sinai Covenant.

3. If God created the universe over billions of years "in the beginning," what was He doing in "the week" that is recounted in the rest of Genesis 1?

The work of God recounted in Genesis 1:2–2:4a falls within a time period of just one week. In that single week we see God preparing "the land" as a suitable habitat for the man and woman He will create on the sixth day. The "land" which the author has in mind is the land promised to Israel (Genesis 15:18). It is there that God prepared the garden of Eden where He could enjoy fellowship with humankind, with those He created in His own image.

God does not *create* "the land" in Genesis 1:2–2:4a; He has already created the land and the rest of the universe "in the beginning" in Genesis 1:1. In the remainder of the chapter, God is at work *preparing* the land for human habitation. As the narrative opens, "the land" is covered by water, and darkness blankets all the water. God brings light and dry land and fills it with fruit trees and animals. By the sixth day, "the land" is a suitable place for the man and the woman to dwell.

Moses thus wants us to see God as both the Creator of the universe (Genesis 1:1) and the Giver of "the land" (Genesis 1:2–2:4). He is the One who created and prepared the land, and He will give it to whomever He pleases. Such a view of God is central to the theology of the Pentateuch and its focus on the Sinai Covenant (Exodus 19:5).

4. If God created the whole of the universe "in the beginning" in Genesis 1:1, then why does He need to create the sun, moon, and stars on the fourth day? Why does He need to create the plants and animals on the third and fifth days?

This question poses a real problem, regardless of how one interprets Genesis 1. The truth is, *every* interpretation faces essentially these same questions.

Though our English translations of Genesis 1 often suggest that God created the sun, moon, and stars on the fourth day, the Hebrew text does

Early biblical chronologies uniformly assumed the world was created only a few thousand years ago. According to traditional Judaism, the year 1996 is 5,756 years after the creation. In the seventeenth century, Bishop Ussher dated creation at 4004 B.C.

Those early attempts at an absolute chronology of the world were not based on Genesis 1 as much as they were on the genealogies of Genesis 5 and 10. By adding the respective ages of the men in those genealogies — the number of years between Adam and Noah and Abraham — they expected to arrive at the total number of years since the creation.

Such an approach to dating the time of creation is based on two faulty assumptions:

1. It assumes that the biblical genealogies are to be understood as strict chronologies.

2. It assumes that the "beginning" of creation (Genesis 1:1) occurred on the first day of the week recounted in that chapter (Genesis 1:2–31).

First, it is now generally recognized that the genealogies in Genesis 5 and 10 are not intended as strict chronologies. Over a hundred years ago one of America's greatest evangelical theologians, Benjamin Breckinridge Warfield, argued that large gaps were to be assumed in those genealogies and "for aught we know instead of twenty generations and some two thousand years measuring the interval between the creation and the birth of Abraham, two hundred generations, and something like twenty thousand years, or even two thousand generations and something like two hundred thousand years may have intervened."[1]

Second, the Hebrew text of Genesis 1 does not have the word "first." That word was added by the translators. Many English versions have rendered the summary in Genesis 1:5 as "and there was evening, and there was morning — the first day" (NIV). By using the phrase "the first day," they imply that no day preceded this one, that this was the "first day" of creation. Yet the Hebrew text reads "and there was evening, and there was morning — one day." The first day of this week, in other words, was not necessarily the first day of creation. It was simply "one day."

The most natural reading of the text of Genesis 1 is that the phrase "it was evening and it was morning, one day" refers to the evenings and mornings (and hence days) of our everyday lives. That, in fact, is how the passage was interpreted within the Pentateuch itself (see Exodus 20:11).

not demand, *or even allow for*, such an interpretation. The overall sense of Genesis 1 assumes that by the fourth day, the sun, moon, and stars are already in place. Moreover, according to the Hebrew text only "fruit trees" were created on the third day, not "all kinds of trees" as many English translations suggest. Those "fruit trees" were for the man's and woman's nourishment (Genesis 1:29).

At the conclusion of the chapter, other plants are mentioned that also are for the nourishment of human beings, as well as food for the animals (Genesis 1:30). Yet the creation of those plants is not mentioned anywhere in the first chapter; clearly they are not created on the third day. Only "fruit trees" were created at that time. The account thus assumes that such plants already were present in God's world. This means that all these things were created as part of "the heavens and earth" in Genesis 1:1.

5. What does this interpretation say about the origin of the human race? Were human beings also created "in the beginning"? If so, why are they created again on the sixth day? Are there two kinds of human beings — those created "in the beginning" and those created on the sixth day?

Human life did not originate until the sixth day of the week recorded in Genesis 1:2–2:4a. That means that human beings were *not* created "in the beginning" with the rest of God's creation. Human beings were "late-comers" according to the biblical account. They came only after the indefinite period of time denoted by the term "beginning."

The genealogy of Adam recorded in Genesis 5 makes it clear that all humanity stems from the single man and woman created in Genesis 1:26–27. Genesis insists that all human beings as we know them are descendants of Adam. That rules out the creation of human beings "in the beginning" in Genesis 1:1. It is an essential part of the logic of the genealogies in chapters 5 and 10 that no human beings were a part of the universe created "in the beginning." Rather, they were created as part of God's work in preparing the "land." All human beings can be traced back to the first man and woman created when God prepared the garden of Eden.

Such a viewpoint fits well with what modern science tells us of early human life. Human life is quite recent in geological history. Clear traces of human beings date back only about thirty thousand years ago, appearing without any discernible antecedents, as if they came from nowhere.

As far as the biblical record is concerned, nothing in Genesis 1 and 2 contradicts modern science. According to the Bible — just as in modern scientific theories — human beings arrived on the scene very recently in geological history, fully developed culturally and linguistically.

6. Where do we put the dinosaurs? Were they created "in the beginning," or were they created on the fifth or sixth day?

The Bible allows for the creation of dinosaurs and all other forms of early plant and animal life "in the beginning," since the Hebrew word for "beginning" in Genesis 1:1 could encompass eons during which God's work of creation was carried out.

Yet there is no reason to suggest that God's work of creation followed the course outlined by modern evolutionary theory. The theory of evolution, especially in its classical Darwinian form, has undergone fundamental challenges and adjustments in recent years. As long as it maintains that God was not or could not have been a factor in the process, it falls under the critique of the first statement of the Bible: "*God* created the heavens and the earth."

Genesis 1:1 allows for (but does not require) a vast period of time during which *God* was at work in the world, creating new species of animals and allowing others to fall into extinction. Like all other examples of God's work of creation, we can see something of His workmanship in the results. The surviving bones and traces of the vast array of animal and plant life from earth's past stand as a striking testimony to the nature of God's work "in the beginning."

IN SUMMARY: LET THE TEXT LEAD THE WAY

Let's summarize the main foundation stones we've just placed.

In trying to understand the creation account in Genesis 1 and 2, we should be guided by what the text itself says, not by attempts to reconcile the text with the ever-changing views of modern science. Once we grasp a clear picture of Genesis 1 and 2, we can then apply their meaning to the important questions which modern science raises.

I believe the interpretation offered in this book provides plausible and coherent answers to many, if not all, of the central questions facing modern readers of the Bible. It does so, moreover, without seriously contradicting scientific facts or making unwarranted concessions to mere scientific theory.

While the conclusions I reach may be markedly different from "traditional" interpretations, they are solidly based in the text itself and have much in common with the work of accomplished Bible scholars from past eras. Even though their views are old, we will see that they have a lot to say to us. They might even prompt us to reconsider the way we read Genesis 1 and 2.

PART TWO

GENESIS RECONSIDERED

• "The beginning" in Genesis 1:1 speaks of an indeterminate period of time, not a single moment of time. God did not have to create the world in a single point of time, but according to the text may have created the world over a rather lengthy period.

• The author's choice of the word "beginning" allowed him to say that God created everything, without going into the details. It thus left him free to concentrate on God's work of preparing the promised land during the six days recorded in the rest of the chapter.

IN THE BEGINNING

hat a difference a word makes! Mark Twain once said the difference between the "right" word and the "almost right" word was the difference between "lightning" and "the lightning bug." How right he was! Pick the wrong word, and instead of holding a jar of phosphorescent insects to light up a summer's night, you wind up with a million volts charring your hand.

How important it is to choose the right word to express a key concept. How crucial it is to avoid the "almost right" word. And how appropriate it is that one of the most crucial words in the entire Genesis creation account is the word "beginning."

What a freight of meaning we have poured into this little word! When we read "In the beginning God created the heavens and the earth," our minds naturally race back to the first moment of time and try to imagine the unimaginable: What was it like in that instant when everything we see around us came into being? Before that moment — nothing. Afterward — a universe to explore. What was it like?

Thoughts like those often course through our brains when we read or hear Genesis 1:1. Yet there may be a problem with such a mental picture: What if it's based on an error? What if we have misunderstood? What if such a picture is not at all what the original author had in mind?

I ask such questions because I firmly believe we may have imported into this little word a meaning which Moses never meant to convey. And if

I'm right, our error may have caused us to misconstrue much of the remainder of the Genesis account.

This chapter is crucial to the argument of the book. So let's get started... at the beginning!

Throughout history, certain key questions have determined our understanding of the biblical text. The meaning of the phrase translated "in the beginning" is among the most important of those questions.

Moses makes it clear in Genesis 1:1 that God created the universe "in the beginning." His chronological note tells us that the creation of the universe preceded all of God's other actions with and in the world. By using the term "beginning," Moses refers to the first of all that God was about to do in the Pentateuch and the Bible. Creation was the start of God's activities, not the conclusion.

Yet what did Moses mean by choosing this particular term? What does it literally mean? What kind of "beginning" did Moses have in mind? And is it possible that we have misunderstood what he wanted to convey?

The Hebrew word *reshit*, which is the term for "beginning" used in this chapter, has a very specific sense in Scripture. In the Bible the term always refers to an extended, yet indeterminate duration of time — *not* a specific moment. It is a block of time which precedes an extended series of time periods. It is a "time before time." The term does not refer to a point in time but to a *period* or *duration* of time which falls before a series of events.

UNLIMITED DURATION OF TIME   SEQUENCE OF TIME

"THE BEGINNING"

To get a feeling for what this term conveys, it may be helpful to look at how it was used in other places in Scripture.

In Job 8:7 the word *reshit* refers to the early part of Job's life, before his misfortunes overtook him. During this time Job grew into full maturity, raised his family, and gained renown for his great wisdom and prosperity. It was an unspecified, but lengthy, period in Job's life.

Within the Book of Genesis itself, the author uses the term *reshit* to refer to the early part of Nimrod's kingdom (Genesis 10:10). The NIV translates *reshit* in that verse as "the first centers [*reshit*] of his kingdom were Babylon, Erech, Adda, and Calneh...."

When the Bible speaks of the reigns of Israel's kings, the word *reshit* is used in a unique reckoning system. The first period of a king's reign usually was not counted as part of the official length of his reign. An unspecified period was allowed during which the king actually reigned, but it was not officially counted as part of his reign. After that period — whatever its duration — the years of the king's reign were counted in consecutive order.

No one knows for certain the origin of this system of reckoning, but we know it was practiced throughout the ancient Near East. To calculate the duration of a king's reign, scribes started to count years only after an initial period of time, which sometimes was only a few months and at other times was several years. This indeterminate period of time before the official reckoning of a king's reign was called "the beginning [*reshit*] of his reign."[1]

"THE BEGINNING OF THE REIGN OF KING ZEDEKIAH"	THE REIGN OF KING ZEDEKIAH
"THE BEGINNING"	YEARS 1 2 3 4 5 6 7 8 9 10...

It was common in ancient Israel to begin counting the years of a king's reign from the first of the year — that is, the first day of the month of Nisan. If the king assumed office prior to that day, as was frequently the case, the time which preceded the first of the year was not reckoned as part of his reign. That time was called "the beginning" (*reshit*). In a few biblical cases "the beginning" of a king's reign amounted to several years. According to Jeremiah 28:1, for example, the "beginning" of King Zedekiah's reign included events which happened four years after he had assumed the throne. In this case the NIV translated the word "beginning" simply as "early in the reign of Zedekiah."

The important point to note is that throughout the Bible the Hebrew term for "beginning" (*reshit*) is the same word used for "the beginning" of the reign of a king. It is also the same word used for the "beginning" in Genesis 1:1, so the author apparently had in mind a "beginning" that was longer than a mere moment. Otherwise, he would have chosen a different term (see "Other Beginnings" below).

Such an understanding of the term "beginning" is essential to appreciating the meaning of the first verse of Genesis. When understood in this way, the text does not say that God created the universe in the first moment of time; rather it says that God created the universe during an indeterminate period of time before the actual reckoning of a sequence of time began. In Genesis 1, the period which follows "the beginning" is a single, seven-day week, which itself is followed by a vast history of humanity, leading ultimately to Abraham and the people of Israel.

Clearly the writer's concern in Genesis 1 is not the time covered by "the beginning." He is content to leave that unspecified. Rather, he is interested in the period which follows "the beginning." To that period he gives a precise framework, beginning on the first day of the first recorded week and thereafter marked off by the six remaining days of Genesis 1 and 2.

The writer of Genesis uses the same system of reckoning time as was used later for the chronologies of Israel's kings. The author's reckoning of a seven-day week is preceded by an indefinite period of time which he calls the "beginning" (*reshit*). The general chronological framework of the first chapter is illustrated in the following chart:

"THE BEGINNING OF CREATION"   "ONE WEEK"

"THE BEGINNING"   DAYS • 1   2   3   4   5   6   7

OTHER BEGINNINGS

It is important to realize that other Hebrew words were available to the author to convey the temporal concept of a "beginning." In fact, throughout the Pentateuch the author uses other Hebrew words to express such a concept. Yet here, at the opening of the book, is the only time he uses this particular word.[2]

The author could have used a Hebrew word for "beginning" similar to the English word "start" or "initial point" (for example, *rishonah* or *techillah*). Had he used one of those words, we would have to translate Genesis 1:1 something like this: "The first thing God did was to create the universe." Using such a term would have *required* that the universe be created in the first moment of time. The diagram below shows what sense Genesis 1:1 would have if another Hebrew word for "beginning" had been chosen.

↓ "THE BEGINNING"

TIME

Many readers today understand Genesis 1:1 in this sense. Why? Because the English word "beginning" suggests that sense. The English translation, "In the beginning God created the heavens and the earth" suggests that in an instant, in a brief moment of time, the whole of the world we see around us came into existence.

I have a good friend who, based on the English translation of Genesis 1:1, is convinced that God created the whole universe in a fraction of a single second. He explains his view by saying that at the first moment of creation everything came into being instantly, but operated as if it had been there for millions or billions of years. Trees were created instantly with rings showing years of growth. The rings of the trees in a particular area had a similar growth pattern, as if they had been through the same summers and winters (which had never taken place). My friend even imagines that in the instant of creation, millions of homing pigeons must have been flying all around the world, returning to homes they had, in fact, never been to. At those homes there must have been nests which they didn't build and squabs which had hatched from eggs that had never been laid. Of course I think my friend's interpretation of Genesis 1:1 is wrong. But if the Hebrew word *reshit* did mean a point in time (which it doesn't), then his understanding would be correct.

A "point in time" interpretation of the term "beginning" is often connected to the "Big Bang" theory. According to this theory, the universe came into existence in a massive explosion of a small, superdense particle of matter. The microsecond of the "Big Bang," during which the universe was set into motion, is taken to be "the beginning" spoken of in Genesis 1:1.

Such an understanding of Genesis 1:1 would be possible with the English word "beginning." It may even be possible with certain other Hebrew words which could be translated "beginning."[3] Such a concept, however, is not likely to be connected with *reshit*, the Hebrew word actually used in Genesis 1:1.

The writer of Genesis 1 did not intend to say that God created the universe in the first moment or split second of time. Rather, the text says that God created the universe during an indeterminate time period, perhaps long before the "promised land" was made habitable and human beings were created. The following drawing shows the relationship between the "beginning" and the one week during which God prepared the promised land for mankind.

GOD CREATED THE UNIVERSE GENESIS 1:1	COD PREPARED THE PROMISED LAND GENESIS 1:2-2:4A
"THE BEGINNING"	"ONE WEEK"
(BILLIONS OF YEARS)	1 2 3 4 5 6 7 (24 HOUR) DAYS

If we were to relate the word *reshit* to contemporary theories of the origin of the universe, we could say the "beginning" may have included a "Big Bang," but it also could have entailed a much longer period of time following the initial explosion, including the time when the dust had settled and the world as we know it had come into being. The word the author chose to use suggests the "beginning" may have covered a time period of considerable length.

THE END AND THE BEGINNING

In opening his account of creation with the phrase "in the beginning," the author has identified the creation as a prelude to the history of God's dealings with humanity. This is the beginning of something great — a history in which God comes to have fellowship with mankind.

A great biblical scholar of the last century, Franz Delitzsch, put it well when he wrote about Genesis 1:1, "Hence will here be the beginning of the history which follows.... The history to be related from this point onwards has heaven and earth for its object, its scenes, its factors. At the head of this history stands the creation of the world as its commencement, or at all events its foundation."[4]

The beginning of history, however, is not the only concern of the author. By commencing his history with a reference to such a beginning, the author has not only begun the history of God and His people, he has also prepared the way for the consummation of that very history at "the end of time." As many biblical scholars have noted, the concept of a "beginning" includes the idea of an "end." There is an eschatology, a view of "last things," already in the first words of the Bible. One scholar has said, "Already in Genesis 1:1 the concept of 'the last days' fills the mind of the reader."[5] The growing focus within the biblical canon on the times of the "end" is an appropriate extension of the "end" already anticipated in the "beginning" of Genesis 1:1.

The fundamental principle suggested in Genesis 1:1 and the prophetic vision of the times of the end in the rest of Scripture is that the "last things will be like the first things."[6] As the prophet Isaiah later foresaw about the "last days," the Lord says, "Behold, I create new heavens and a new earth" (Isaiah 65:17; cf. Revelation 21:1: "And I saw a new heaven and a new earth"). The allusions to Genesis 1 and 2 in Revelation 22 illustrate the role these early chapters of Genesis have played in shaping the form and content of the scriptural vision of the future.

Therefore, with the use of the word "beginning," the author establishes that God has a plan and a purpose. A "beginning" to God's actions implies a continuation of those actions and ultimately a conclusion. The world is thus a part of a divine plan. History is a part of the plan and is moving towards its conclusion.

The author of Genesis was a master wordsmith. He chose his words with care and used them with precision. It was no accident or mere happenstance that he picked the Hebrew word *reshit* to begin his narrative of God's dealings with the world and with humankind. He did not want us to focus on the method or process God used to create the stars and sun and moon and earth, but rather intended to draw our attention to God's special preparation of the land as a place for humankind to dwell in safety.

The term *reshit* was particularly appropriate for such a task. Using it allowed the author to insist that the covenant God alone created all that is, even while it permitted him to focus our attention specifically on the time period that followed.

Of course, the author's careful use of vocabulary and phraseology was not restricted to the critical term *reshit*. As we are about to see, modern authors could learn a lot from him about effective word choice.

HISTORICAL CREATIONISM

I believe the name "Historical Creationism" best describes the view of Genesis 1 and 2 presented in this book. This view is a form of "creationism" because it understands Genesis 1 and 2 to be a literal and realistic account of God's creation of the universe. It holds that these chapters teach that God created the universe "out of nothing" (*creatio ex nihilo*, see Appendix 2). There are no "gaps" in the creation account of Genesis 1, nor is there a "re-creation" or "restitution" of an original creation. I believe Genesis 1 and 2 teach that God created the whole universe during a time which the writer calls "the beginning." That "beginning" was not a point of time but a period of time — in all likelihood, a long period of time. After that period of time, God went on to prepare the "land" as a place for human beings to dwell.

By calling this view "Historical Creationism," I distinguish it from other forms of "creationism" such as "Scientific Creationism." The term "historical" distinguishes this view from "Scientific Creationism" in three important ways.

First, my view does not start from the assumption that modern science holds the answer to the meaning of the biblical text. On the contrary, I believe we must first understand the biblical text and then seek to relate its meaning to the findings of modern science, if possible. In this sense, my view might also be called "Textual Creationism." It focuses on the meaning of the biblical author as expressed in the biblical text.

Second, the term "historical" points to the fact that this view of the Genesis creation account can be traced back to a way of reading Genesis 1 and 2 that flourished before the rise of science and its use in biblical interpretation. Before progress in navigation and transportation made global exploration of our world possible, biblical scholars and ordinary people read Genesis 1 within a rather limited geographic scope. It was natural to view the biblical account within the narrow limits of what was known about the world. More precisely, what was known about the world was gathered not from actual exploration, but from both the Bible and the speculations of ancient geographers. Medieval maps of the world testify to this fact. The world was thought of as a single body of land surrounded by a large body of water. In such maps of the world, the "promised land," with Jerusalem at its center, was envisioned as the center of the inhabited world. The "Table of Nations" in Genesis 10, which recounts the places inhabited by the descendants of Noah's three sons, was taken as a description of the inhabited world. Apparently little thought was given to the fact that Genesis 10 described only the immediate environs of the promised land. Thus, in the days before the discoveries of the "New World" and beyond, the limited geographical horizons of the readers of the Bible fit well into the geographical focus of the biblical authors. Consequently, my view is often found in earlier works.

Third, the term "historical" points to the fact that in my view of Genesis 1 and 2, the author clearly intends us to read his account of creation as literal history. He does not expect to be understood as writing mythology or poetry. His account, as he understands it, is a historical account of creation.

• The Hebrew term commonly rendered "earth" in English translations, more precisely means "land" in Genesis 1. The work of God during the six days of creation, therefore, is an account of His preparing "the promised land" as a place for man and woman to dwell.

• The Hebrew word "heavens" is more properly rendered "sky." It is the whole of the region above "the land."

• The Hebrew expression "heavens and earth" is a figure of speech which means "the entire universe."

CHAPTER FOUR

THE LAND AND THE SKY

T he first verse of the Bible confronts us with a number of crucial translation questions. We have already looked at the first, the precise meaning of the term *reshit* ("beginning").

Equally important is our understanding of the Hebrew term "land" (*eretz*) in the first two verses of Genesis and in the remainder of the chapter. Our English versions normally render this term with the word "earth." Though "earth" is certainly a possible translation, it doesn't provide the clearest sense of the term in either Genesis 1 or 2.

WHAT'S THE DIFFERENCE?

The key difference between the English words "land" and "earth" lies in the sense that we commonly give to the word "earth." We think of "earth" as the name of our planet. "Earth" conjures up images of a globe sitting on our desk or a blue disk in space as we might see it from the moon.

As we've said before, modern readers almost always fill ancient words with their own perspectives; we can hardly help but do this. For example, in the Bible the Hebrew word *rakab* means "to ride a horse, a chariot, or a camel." Today, the same word also means "to ride a bicycle." Think of what problems it would create if one read today's meaning of the word back into the biblical passages.

Yet I believe this is precisely what has happened with the term *eretz* in Genesis 1:1–2. We have filled the word with a meaning it clearly did not suggest to its original readers.

The central question we have to answer is the exact meaning of the Hebrew term *eretz* as it is used in verse 1 and in verse 2 (and throughout the rest of the chapter). Does it mean the same thing in both verses? Or could context change its meaning from the first to the second verse?

There are, in fact, good reasons to believe that the meaning of *eretz* is different in verse one than it is in the remainder of the chapter. We'll get to those reasons in a moment. But first, let's focus on the meaning of the term *eretz* as it is used in most of the first few chapters of Genesis. Then we will back up and look at verse one to see what distinguishes it from verse two and the rest of the chapter. Finally we'll summarize our findings and discuss how this understanding helps to clear up some long-standing problems in our reading of the creation account.

DOES ERETZ = LAND?

In some contexts, *eretz* can refer to the "earth" in a global sense. In Genesis 18:25, for example, Abraham called God "the Judge of all the *eretz*." Clearly, the sense of the term here is universal and thus should be translated "earth." Such a global sense of *eretz*, however, is not its primary or most common meaning.[1]

At other times it's difficult to determine whether *eretz* is to be taken in a local or global sense. When the psalmist speaks of the "kings of the land [*eretz*]" who take their stand against the Lord's anointed one (Psalm 2:2), does he mean the "kings of the earth" or the "kings of the land"? Does he mean all the kings of every country throughout the whole earth, or does he have in mind merely the kings who have rebelled against the king of Judah? If Psalm 2 is to be understood in a messianic sense, which is likely, then *eretz* has a global meaning: the whole earth. If its original meaning is not strictly messianic, *eretz* would simply mean "the land" surrounding the realm of the kings of Judah.

Throughout most of Genesis, the term *eretz* refers to the dry ground where the man and the woman were to dwell after they were created. Such is the sense of the term in Genesis 1:10: "God called the dry ground 'land' [*eretz*]." Here, the NIV has correctly rendered the term as "land." From Genesis 1:2 on, the focus of the creation account is on that special place where human beings, God's special creatures, are to dwell — the "land."

"Land" is a better translation than "earth" for the Hebrew term *eretz* because the term "land" extends only to what we see of the earth around us, what is within our horizons. The land is the dry ground where the man and the woman were to dwell when they were created. It is this sense that most closely approximates the Hebrew word *eretz* in Genesis 1:2.

Throughout Genesis 1, the term *eretz* is used to denote "the dry land," as opposed to a body of water, the seas (1:10). The "seas" do not cover the "land," as would be the case if the term meant "earth." Rather the "seas" lie adjacent to the "land" and within it.

Furthermore, "the land" is commanded to sprout forth fruit trees (1:11). Here the sense is clearly akin to our words "soil" or "ground." In Genesis 1, the birds fly "over the land" (1:20), and the "land" is commanded to bring forth livestock and wild animals (1:24), just as the "waters" are commanded to bring forth the fish (1:20). The land animals are here contrasted with sea creatures. As the fish are told to "fill the waters," so mankind is told to "fill the land and subdue it" (1:28). The general meaning of the term "land" in Genesis 1 can thus be visualized in the following manner:

This view of the land, seen throughout Genesis 1, appears to be the same as that in Exodus 20, which frequently alludes back to Genesis 1. In Exodus 20, the world is described in three major segments, "the sky, the land, and the waters below the land" (20:4). The sense of the term "land" in that passage is clearly local and geographical. It's not describing the "earth" floating on "the waters below it." It rather pictures the sky above, the land below, and the waters running their courses beneath the land.

The passage that describes the "naming" of the land (Genesis 1:10) is crucial to our understanding this term throughout the creation account. Here the "land" is specifically contrasted with the "seas." The land is the "dry ground" raised above the seas — just as in Genesis 1:2 the land is the ground that lies under the sea. In both contexts, the land is defined by its contrast with the seas, not by its contrast with the stars and planets.

To summarize, the usual meaning of *eretz* is simply "the land" and not "the earth" as in most English translations. For the most part, it refers to a specific stretch of land in a local, geographical, or political sense. Often it means simply "the ground" upon which one stands. As such, it is frequently used interchangeably with another common Hebrew word *adamah* (that is, "arable ground").

DOES THE LAND = THE PROMISED LAND?

Not only does the Hebrew term *eretz* normally mean "land" as opposed to "the earth," but it usually refers specifically to the land promised to Abraham (Genesis 15:18). Certainly the term doesn't always denote "the promised land." It may be "the land" of Egypt (Exodus 1:7) or simply the place of one's birth, the "homeland" (Genesis 12:1). But most often in Genesis and throughout the Pentateuch the term *eretz* refers to the promised land. There are at least four reasons for understanding *eretz* (as it is used in Genesis 1) in this way.

1. *The close relationship between the first two chapters of Genesis supports a localized view of the "land."*

Often the two creation narratives in Genesis 1 and 2 have been thought to be only loosely connected: While Genesis 1 is about God's preparing the earth, Genesis 2 is about the garden. Such a reading, however, misses an important point. In their present placement within the Pentateuch, the two narratives are about the *same* events and have the *same* setting. What we see God doing in Genesis 2 is merely another perspective on what He does in Genesis 1. An important implication of such a reading is that the setting of chapter 2, the garden of Eden, is the same as that of chapter 1, the land. Since chapter 2 is clearly an account of God's preparing the garden of Eden as man's dwelling place, chapter 1 must also be about God's preparing the garden.

2. *The biblical location of "the land" with respect to the city of Babylon "in the east" indicates that throughout these narratives the author has in mind the promised land.*

In Genesis 11:1 we are told that all the land had one language with few words. What "land" does the author have in mind here? Most English versions would have us understand this as "the whole earth." Such an interpretation, however, is not as apparent as we might at first think.

The following verse says that "they [the whole earth?] moved eastward and found a valley in the land of Shinar and they dwelt there" (11:2). Only a few verses later (and in Genesis 10:10) we learn that those same people (the whole earth? or the whole land?) dwelt in the land of the city of Babylon. In other words, in Genesis 11:1–2 the people who dwelt in "the land" moved "eastward" and settled in "the land of Shinar." There they built the city of Babylon.

It seems clear from this text that the author did not understand "the land" in Genesis 11:1 as "the whole earth." Rather, it was simply the region west of Babylon. If you traveled east from "the land," you wound up in Babylon.

It is interesting to note the parallels between the story of the building of Babylon (Genesis 11:1–9) and the story of Paradise Lost (Genesis 3:22–24). (Note: "Babel" is the Hebrew name for "Babylon.") Just as the people of the land went eastward from the land and found themselves in

Babylon (11:1–2), so too the first man and woman were cast out of the garden eastward (3:24) as was Cain (Genesis 4:16). This implicit geography within these early narratives locates the promised land centrally and sees movement away from it as "eastward" and away from God's presence, to Babylon. It is thus understood within the narratives that "the land" is in fact the promised land.

Such an understanding is maintained throughout the remainder of the Pentateuch. The entrance to the garden of Eden, and hence the promised land, was guarded by angels or cherubim (Genesis 3:24). Could that be the reason Jacob was met by "the angels of God" as he returned to the promised land from the east (Genesis 32:1–2)? In fact, he had to wrestle with an angel and prevail over him to reenter the land (32:22–32). Joshua was also met by angels as he prepared to reenter the promised land (Joshua 5:13–15).

3. The central theme of the Pentateuch is the Sinai Covenant and God's gift of the land.

In the Sinai Covenant, God vowed to give Israel the land promised to their forefathers (Deuteronomy 1:8). The theme of God's good land and His gift of that land to Israel is central to the Pentateuch. The close ties between the creation narratives in Genesis and the narratives which focus specifically on the covenant[2] suggest they are all concerned with the same general theme: God's gift of the land. Most of the narratives in the Pentateuch are preoccupied with the concept of God's land. Thus, from the start of the creation account, the author betrays his interest in the Sinai Covenant by concentrating our attention on "the land."

In many ways this is the strongest argument for taking the setting of Genesis 1 and 2 as the promised land. A reader familiar with the theme and purpose of the Pentateuch would naturally see the land in Genesis 1 as the promised land. Unfortunately, by not rendering *eretz* in Genesis 1:1–2 as "land," our English translations have blurred the connection of these early verses of Genesis to the central theme of the land in the Pentateuch.

4. Later interbiblical interpretation clearly saw the promised land as the focus of the creation account.

God told Israel through the prophet Jeremiah, "I made the land [*eretz*], mankind, and the animals upon the land with my great and powerful outstretched hand, and I will give it to whomever I please" (Jeremiah 27:5). As the passage then says, God was about to give the "land" to the Babylonian king Nebuchadnezzar (27:6). In fact, God was about to give "all the lands" (*ertzoth*, plural) to Nebuchadnezzar. God was about to give Israel's land and the lands of her neighbors to the Babylonian king.

CREATIONISM

Creationism interprets the biblical account of creation literally. God created the universe in six days. He created man on the sixth day. The universe is quite young, approximately ten thousand years old. The present condition of the earth — which gives the appearance of being much older — reflects the catastrophic destruction wrought by Noah's flood.

The key difficulty in modern scientific explanations of the age of the earth is the notion of "uniformitarianism," the idea that all physical processes have always operated at a uniform rate. According to most scientists, the Grand Canyon would have taken hundreds of thousands of years to be created, since it has always eroded at the same rate which it experiences today. Creationists, on the other hand, believe the Grand Canyon is a result of the receding floodwaters in Noah's day and could have been formed in a matter of weeks or months.

Creationists do not apply their scientific method to the creation account in Genesis 1, but to the flood account in Genesis 6–9. There they rely on principles and experiments related to "fluid dynamics," the study of the laws of water in motion.

They explain the fossil record by the laws of sedimentation. When material settles in a fluid, denser particles tend to settle faster than less dense ones. After the floodwaters had calmed over the earth and dead animals began to sink to the bottom, the smaller, more dense species settled first. This accounts for the basic pattern of the fossil record — smaller crustaceans at the bottom and larger mammals at the top. In this way the fossil record could have been laid down in a matter of weeks, months, or a few years.

No one doubts that in this passage God's "making the land" refers to the creation account in Genesis 1. That it refers to Genesis 1:2–2:4a and not Genesis 1:1 is shown by the fact that Jeremiah used the Hebrew term "to make" (*asah*) and not the term "to create" (*bara*). It is also clear from the context that Jeremiah did not have the "whole earth" in mind when he said God was about to give the land to Babylon. His point was that the land was to be destroyed by Babylon and its people taken away into captivity.

Some English translations of this passage give a different view of Jeremiah's words by rendering the term *eretz* as "earth." In the NIV, for example, God says, "I made the earth and its people and the animals that are on it, and I give it to anyone I please." Yet the passage itself makes it clear that the land God was about to give to Nebuchadnezzar was the same "land" which He had made in Genesis 1. There is no thought in Jeremiah's words that God was about to give the "whole earth" to Nebuchadnezzar. The very next verse says that God was about to give only Judah's land and the lands of her neighbors into the hands of the Babylonian king. The land which God was going to give Nebuchadnezzar was the same land occupied by the nations listed in Jeremiah 27:3 — Edom, Moab, Ammon, Tyre, and Sidon. Thus, when Jeremiah looked back on the creation narrative in Genesis 1, he saw it principally as an account of God's making that very land which He would later take away from Israel and her neighbors and give to Nebuchadnezzar. That land was the promised land.

Later biblical authors also understood Genesis 1 to be principally about the promised land. The prophets consistently identified the promised land with the garden of Eden. The concept of a "return to Eden" in the future was part and parcel of the stock imagery of the prophets (see Isaiah 51:3; Ezekiel 36:35; Joel 2:3). Furthermore, the restoration of the garden of Eden in the promised land is a well-known feature of John's vision in the Book of Revelation (Revelation 21–22).

In Genesis 1, the word "sky" (*shamayim*), by itself, refers to the open space above the land. It is that realm which contains the clouds, the sun, moon, and stars. It was also the place where the birds fly (see Genesis 1:20). Though the word "heavens" has commonly been used to translate the Hebrew word *shamayim*, the word "sky" is often more appropriate. We do not normally think of birds flying "in the heavens." The English word "sky" is preferable because it is a more comprehensive term. It includes both the place where the celestial bodies dwell, as well as the place where the clouds are and the birds fly.

The two words "sky" (*shamayim*) and "land" (*eretz*) are used numerous times in Genesis 1. In each case their meaning is clear from the context. The English words "heavens" and "earth" do not best convey the sense these terms have in Hebrew. As suggested earlier, the sense of the term "land" can be seen most clearly from verse 10: "And God called the dry ground 'land.'" The term "land" (*eretz*) in this verse is the same term translated "earth" (*eretz*) in Genesis 1:1 and 1:2. Within the context of Genesis 1, it is reasonable to suspect that they should have the same meaning.

THE MEANING OF THE PHRASE "HEAVENS AND EARTH"

Now let's consider the meaning of *eretz* in Genesis 1:1. Having just argued for a specific meaning for the terms "sky" and "land" in Genesis 1, it is crucial to see that when these two terms are used together as a figure of speech, they take on a distinct meaning of their own. Together, they mean far more than the sum of the meanings of the two individual words. Let me explain.

When I teach, I often use a blackboard. Yet in most schools where I have taught, the boards were not black at all. Some were green, others were white. If I say to my students that a quiz is written on the blackboard, they all know what I mean. The meaning of "blackboard" is not merely a combination of the words "black" and "board." The two words together mean something quite different than each one separately.

A similar thing is true with the terms "sky" and "land" in Genesis 1:1. They combine to form a figure of speech called a "merism." A merism combines two words to express a single idea. A merism expresses "totality" by combining two contrasts or two extremes.

For example, David says in Psalm 139:2, "O Lord, you know my sitting down and my rising up." This merism means that the Lord knows everything about David. The concept of "everything" is expressed by combining the two opposites "my sitting down" and "my rising up."

In the case of the merism "sky and land," the terms *shamayim* ("sky") and *eretz* ("land") represent two extremes in the world. By linking these two extremes into a single expression — "sky and land" or "heavens and earth" — the Hebrew language expresses the totality of all that exists. Unlike English, Hebrew doesn't have a single word to express the concept of "the universe"; it must do so by means of a merism. The expression "sky and land" thus stands for the "entirety of the universe." It includes not only the two extremes, heaven and earth, but also all that they contain — the sun, the moon, and the stars; every seen and unseen part of the universe; the seas, the dry land, and the plants and animals that inhabit them.

The expression "the sky and the land" looks at the world from the perspective of everyday life. As an observer looks around, the world appears to consist of two major segments, the sky above and the land below. These two components form the basis for thinking about the whole of the universe. The figure below depicts the meaning of the merism "heavens and earth."

THE HEAVENS (SKY)

THE EARTH (LAND)

A proper understanding of the merism "sky and land" has important implications for the meaning of Genesis 1. If Genesis 1:1 really does describe God's creation of the universe, the text must then mean that God created the whole of the universe — including the sun, moon, and stars — "in the beginning." Such an understanding will greatly effect how we interpret the remainder of the first chapter.

If, for example, God created the whole universe in the first verse, then what was He doing in the rest of Genesis 1? The very next verse provides the answer. Genesis 1:2 immediately focuses our attention on "the land." Therefore the rest of the creation account (Genesis 1:2–2:4) is about God's preparing the "land."

TIME FOR A REVIEW

Let's review for a moment. The use of the merism "sky and land" in the Bible focuses specifically on the world *as we know it today*. In Isaiah 44:24, for example, the Lord says, "I, the Lord, made all things. I, alone, stretched out the sky. I, alone, hammered out the land." For Isaiah, "sky and land" are equivalent to "all things" (see also Jeremiah 10:16; Psalm 103:19).

Isaiah is not alone here. The use of the merism "sky and land" throughout Scripture shows that the phrase includes the land, the sun and moon, as well as the stars. In Joel 3:15–16, for example, the phrase "sky and land" includes the "land" of Zion (that is, Jerusalem), as well as all the sky, filled with the sun, moon, and stars above it.

As in any figure of speech, one must be careful to distinguish between the meaning of the words when they occur by themselves and their meaning when they occur within the figure of speech. The terms "land" and "sky" occur by themselves throughout Genesis 1. When not used in a merism, the individual words "sky" and "land" have their own distinct meaning which can be determined from the text.

On the other hand, these two terms occur within the merism "sky and land" only a few times in Genesis. When they so appear, the phrase means "the universe." Such an understanding of the expression "sky and land" helps solve several vexing questions in Genesis 1.

Let's consider one such puzzling question. How are we to think of the "light" in Genesis 1:3 ("And God said, 'Let there be light,' and there was light.")?

Because some interpreters don't appreciate the sense of the expression "sky and land" in Genesis 1:1, they are forced to hold that the "light" in verse 3 was a special form of light which existed before God created the sun.

Yet if the sun is meant to be included in the merism "sky and land" in Genesis 1:1, then it is natural to assume that the sun was created already in the first verse. If that is so, then the "light" of verse 3 is simply the light of the sun. Such an understanding of the phrase appears to be the most natural assumption of the author and also the most natural reading of the text. Though not used frequently in Scripture, the expression "there was light" is one way the Bible refers to sunlight.[3]

When we understand the phrase "sky and land" to include the sun, one of the most intransigent problems of Genesis 1 is resolved. The light in Genesis 1:3 is simply the sunlight. That is also how the "days" mentioned throughout Genesis 1 are to be understood; they are the days marked off by successive sunrises.[4]

IN SUMMARY: LIMITING A RANGE OF MEANING

In this chapter I have tried to show that the meaning of the Hebrew term usually translated "earth" (eretz) is better translated as "land" and is better understood as "the land" promised to Israel.

Whatever the English word "earth" may have meant to the early English translators of the Bible, today it means something quite different than what the biblical writer intended. Today the word "earth" too easily calls up images of the whole planet on which we live, including its oceans, rivers, lakes, and deserts, as well as the great mass of underground strata which make up our world. Most recently, the term "earth" has come to refer even to the whole of the biosphere within which our planet exists;

even the ozone layer which covers our planet is included in the ecological system we call "earth."

The point is that the meaning of biblical terms inevitably expands with modern usage *unless we consciously limit the range of those terms by careful attention to the meaning of the text.* By allowing the term "earth" to expand beyond the limits of the author's own perspective, modern readers of the Bible have missed an important link in the overall meaning of the biblical creation account.

This account both affirms God's creation of the universe (Genesis 1:1) and shows His special concern for the land promised to the patriarchs (Genesis 1:2–2:4a). That concern was so special that the author called unique attention to the labors God expended in preparing the land. We would be wise to try to understand how the writer did this.

• Modern English translations of Genesis 1:1 carry a lot of baggage from an earlier time when the Bible was made to conform to Greek conceptions of the origin of the universe.

• Viewed from the perspective of the Hebrew text, the phrase "formless and void" means simply "uninhabitable land."

CHAPTER FIVE

FORMLESS AND VOID?

odern translations of the Bible are not always as "modern" as you might think. The New International Version of the Holy Bible, for example — the best-selling English translation in America — was first released in a complete edition in 1978, with a revised version following in 1983. Yet its rendering of Genesis 1:2 reflects a tradition and an understanding thousands of years old — and one which could lead to a quite serious misunderstanding.

AN OLD TRADITION

William Tyndale in 1530 was the first English translator to render the Hebrew phrase *tohu wabohu* in Genesis 1:2 with the expression "void and empty." Tyndale's translation has had a lasting effect. The King James Bible (1611) and the Geneva Bible (1560) both rendered it "without form and void." That basic idea still predominates today with translations such as the NIV's "formless and empty."

Although Tyndale was the first to popularize this idea in an English Bible, his translation was far from original. A good deal of interpretation was packed into his rendering of that phrase. His translation, as well as that of the King James Bible, the Geneva Bible, and the NIV, were *learned* translations.

Though the phrase may suggest many things to modern readers, the early English translators had precise intentions for the expression "formless and void." They used it to harmonize the biblical creation account with the prevailing Greek cosmology of their day (see Part Four for an extended discussion of this issue). They expressly meant to say that God did not originally create the world in the condition in which we now see it. Instead, He created the universe as a shapeless mass of material, only later forming the world we now know.

In effect, these translators saw two creations. In the first creation of Genesis 1:1, God created the raw materials of the universe. In the second creation of Genesis 1:2–2:4a, God gave shape and form to the earlier primeval mass.

The translators did have to adapt the Greek view in one major area. While the Greeks held that matter was eternal, the Bible insists that God created the universe "out of nothing." Yet after modifying the Greek idea in that way, translators immediately fell back on the idea of a primeval, formless mass. When God created the world, they argued, it was at first only a formless mass of matter. Later God gave shape and order to that "formless and void" mass. In this way, the biblical account of creation could be shown to be "true" because it conformed to the generally accepted Greek cosmologies.

These early English versions mirrored what others had been doing for centuries. More than fifteen hundred years before Tyndale, the Septuagint had translated the Hebrew expression *tohu wabohu* with the Greek terms meaning "unseen" and "unformed." The 1560 Geneva Bible's "without forme and void" reflected John Calvin's own translation.[1] Calvin wrote about Genesis 1:2 that "were we now to take away, I say, from the earth all that God added after the time here alluded to, then we should have this rude and unpolished, or rather shapeless chaos."[2]

YOU'VE COME A LONG WAY, BABY — OR HAVE YOU?

While today's readers and translators of Genesis 1 have left far behind the ancient Greek idea of a primeval, chaotic mass, they attach new significance to the phrase "without form and void." For example, when a modern reader comes across the words "formless and empty" in Genesis 1, he or she quite often thinks of the earth and the universe as a scientist might describe its early stages — a mass of cooling gases, whirling through space, evolving into its present shape.

What often comes to mind when I read the English text is a lamp my family had when I was a kid. You still see such lamps in novelty shops (I even understand they're making a comeback). The "lava lamps." A light bulb is located beneath a glass container filled with colored water and a viscous, fatty-like substance. As the bulb heats up, the viscous material moves about the container in a constantly changing, amorphous mass. It is "without form and void."

Today the phrase "formless and void" calls up images from astronomy and modern science textbooks instead of images borrowed from Greek cosmologies. The New Scofield Bible (1967), for example, says the phrase "formless and void" describes "an original formless matter in the first stage of the creation of the universe."[3] The astronomer Hugh Ross sees in the terms "formless and void" the state of the earth just after it had condensed from a primordial ball of gases.[4]

Although these pictures can find support in the English expression "without form and void," they are unlikely to arise out of the original Hebrew phrase *tohu wabohu*. Were it not for the Greek notion of "primeval chaos," the phrase never would have been translated that way. The sense of the Hebrew phrase suggests something quite different, a sense which some early translators identified quite clearly.

A VOID OR A WILDERNESS?

The early Jewish-Greek translations by men such as Aquila ("empty and nothing") and Symmachus ("fallow and indistinct") decidedly moved away from the translation of the Septuagint. In doing so they showed a closer affinity to other early Jewish interpreters. The early non-Greek versions such as the Aramaic Targums show no trace of the concepts found in the Septuagint. We know, for example, that an early Aramaic Targum of Genesis 1 known as Neophyti I paraphrased the expression in Genesis 1:2

by rendering it "desolate without human beings or beasts and void of all cultivation of plants and of trees." Rather than "formless and empty," such a translation conveys the idea of "uninhabitable" and "wilderness" — the correct sense of the Hebrew phrase.

According to the most natural reading of the Hebrew text, the land was simply an "uninhabitable" or "inhospitable" stretch of "wasteland." The land was not a "formless and empty chaos." When God made the world, the land was not yet a place where human beings could dwell (Genesis 1:2). It had not yet been prepared for their habitation. That, of course, is a quite different sense than the phrases "formless and empty" (NIV) or "without form and void" (RSV) might imply!

The Hebrew expression *tohu wabohu* refers simply to a "wilderness" that has not yet become inhabitable for human beings. It is the "wilderness," for example, where the Israelites wandered for forty years, waiting to enter the land (Deuteronomy 32:10).

Such a meaning for the Hebrew expression fits quite well into the context of Genesis 1. Throughout this chapter God is depicted as preparing the land for man's habitation. Through the hand of God, the "wasteland" is about to become the "promised land."

The immediate context of Genesis 1 (1:2a, 9) suggests that the land was described as "formless and empty" primarily because "darkness" was upon the land and the land was "covered with water." For those reasons the land was "uninhabitable." The general context of chapter 1 would indicate that the author meant the terms *tohu wabohu* to describe the condition of the land before God made it "good."

Even a quick reading of the Hebrew text reveals an obvious wordplay between the terms *tohu* ("deserted") and *tob* ("good"). Before God began His work, the land was "deserted" (*tohu*); then God made it "good" (*tob*).

In this sense, the description of the land in 1:2 is similar to the description of the land in 2:5–6. Both texts describe the land as "not yet" what it shall be. Having described the land as uninhabitable, the remainder of Genesis 1 portrays God as preparing the land for the place of man's dwelling.[5] The description of the land as *tohu wabohu* in verse 2a, then, plays a central role in the creation account. It describes the condition of the land before God's gracious work prepared it for man's dwelling place.

FROM THE WILDERNESS TO THE PROMISED LAND

At the close of the Pentateuch, Deuteronomy draws on this very imagery (32:10) to depict Israel's time of waiting in the "wilderness" before their entry into the "good land." God's people must go through the *wilderness* to reach the *promised land*.

The prophets drew from the same source to picture God's judgment of exile upon His disobedient people. When Israel disobeyed God, the land again became "uninhabitable" (*tohu*), and the people were sent into exile.

After the time of exile, the prophet Jeremiah said of Israel's land: "I looked at the land and it was formless and empty (*tohu wabohu*) and at the heavens and their light was gone...the fruitful land was a desert" (Jeremiah 4:23–26). Note that the promised land after the exile is described in precisely the same terms chosen earlier to picture the land before God prepared it for mankind at creation — *not* "void and empty," but "deserted and uninhabited."

IN SUMMARY: CRUCIAL WORDS

No set of words characterizes the role of the Bible translators in shaping our understanding of Genesis 1 and 2 more than the terms "formless and void" (*tohu wabohu*). The phrase was chosen not so much because it was the best translation of the Hebrew words but rather because it could be used to identify the "heavens and earth" in Genesis 1:1 with a primeval chaos.

Its common meaning throughout the Hebrew Scriptures, however, suggests that the phrase should be understood as "wilderness, devoid of human life." It is that stretch of land not "good" for human beings. The point of the biblical author was that the land needed further preparation before God could place human beings upon it. Once that occurred, the land would no longer be a wilderness, devoid of human life, but could be pronounced "good" for the man and the woman. In fact, you might say it would become a regular garden of Eden.

• The writer of Genesis has identified the "land" prepared in Genesis 1 with the garden of Eden described in Genesis 2.

• The garden of Eden anticipates the tabernacle where God desired to dwell with his chosen people.

• Adam and Eve, like the later Israelites, could enjoy God's great provision of the "land" as long as they were obedient.

• The notion of God's preparing the "land" for Adam and Eve plays a central role in the larger plan and purpose of the writer of the Pentateuch.

CHAPTER SIX

THE GARDEN OF EDEN

In many ways the picture of God's preparation of the garden of Eden for the newly created man and woman epitomizes all that Genesis 1 and 2 intend to say about God's purposes in creation. It is the jewel in the larger setting of the creation narrative.

God created the garden as a fit place for the man and woman to dwell and to have fellowship with Him. Viewed from the context of the entire Pentateuch, the garden of Eden foreshadows the tabernacle where Israel was to meet with God. At least two major parallels exist:

• Just as Israel was to take the tabernacle with them as they entered the promised land and there they would meet with God, so the garden lay in the midst of the land in Genesis 1 and 2, and there Adam and Eve were to meet with God.

• As long as Adam and Eve were obedient to God's will, they could enjoy God's good provisions. But when they disobeyed God and ate of the Tree of Knowing Good and Evil, God cast them out of the garden "eastward," in the direction of the city of Babylon (Genesis 11). So also God warned Israel that if they were disobedient, they too would be cast out of the land, "eastward" into the city of Babylon.

As we are about to see, there are also many other reasons for believing that Genesis 1:2b–2:4 identifies the garden of Eden with the promised land.

The word "Eden" appears to denote a specific place. In the Hebrew Bible, the word usually means "delight." We may assume the name was intended to evoke a picture of idyllic delight and rest.

An inordinate amount of attention is devoted in chapter 2 to the description of the garden. In the garden we find beautiful, lush fruit trees, including the elusive "tree of life" and "tree of the knowledge of good and evil." We also find a river that divides into four "head streams." Special care is given to locate the rivers and to describe the lands through which they flow, lands rich in gold and precious jewels.

We are told that the Lord God planted the garden "in Eden to the east," and this fact is striking. Elsewhere in the Book of Genesis "eastward" is associated with judgment and separation from God (see 3:24; 11:2; 13:11). Moreover, when the man and woman were expelled from the garden, the cherubim were placed "on the east" (3:24) of the garden, giving the impression that the garden itself was not in the east.

Such an apparent difficulty in the flow of the narrative may account for the fact that in 2:8 the garden is not actually called the "garden of Eden," as it is elsewhere, but rather the "garden in Eden" — a designation found only in verse 8. Thus, the garden was planted in Eden, which was apparently a site larger than the garden itself. If the phrase "on the east" refers to Eden itself, the garden was on its eastern side.[1]

LOCATION OF THE GARDEN

For the most part, questions about the location of the garden of Eden have centered on physical explorations of the Near East. Many ancient and modern explorers have risked life and limb in search of the garden of Eden and the Tree of Life.[2]

Our concern here, however, is not with the physical location of the garden of Eden but with the textual identity of the garden. Where is the biblical writer telling us the garden was located? Can the borders of the garden of Eden given in Genesis 2 be identified with any other specific area within the subsequent Genesis narratives? I believe the answer is yes; the author of these narratives had a specific place in mind when he spoke of the garden of Eden. That place is the promised land.

The location of the garden of Eden is identified textually by four rivers. The relationship of the four rivers that flowed out of the garden (Genesis 2:10b–14) and the single river from which they originated (Genesis 2:10a) is difficult to reconstruct, and perhaps impossible. Two of the four rivers mentioned (Genesis 2:8–14) can be identified with certainty: the Euphrates and the Tigris. The other two, the Pishon and the Gihon, are more difficult to identify, although we are given clues. The identification of the Pishon remains a textual mystery since the land of Havilah, through which it flowed, cannot be identified.[3]

PROGRESSIVE CREATIONISM

Progressive creationists teach that God created the universe in the beginning. The universe is some eight to fifteen billion years old, and life on earth began some three and a half billion years ago. The biblical account of Adam and Eve is historical and can be dated prior to the first traces of human life, about twenty to fifty thousand years ago. Thus, God created the first man and woman; they did not evolve from apes.

Yet the account of creation in Genesis 1 should not be taken strictly literally. Either the days are to be thought of as long ages of time, or the whole account is to be understood as a picturesque story which teaches about real acts of God but doesn't literally depict those acts. Many progressive creationists attempt to show that the word "day" in Genesis 1 was not intended to be understood as a twenty-four-hour day.

Progressive creationists, like "scientific" creationists, use modern scientific methods in their interpretation of the Bible. They rely on scientific dating methods for establishing the age of the universe, the earth, and life on earth. They read Genesis 1 as if it were a blueprint for modern geological theories. The "days" of Genesis 1 represent the geological "ages" of modern geology. The order of events in Genesis 1 parallels the sequences of the formation of the physical universe. For the most part, progressive creationists apply their scientific viewpoints to the creation of the earth in Genesis 1, while creationists apply it to the flood in Genesis 6–9.

The garden of Eden extended from the "river that flows through all the land of Cush" to the "River Euphrates." Since in Genesis the land of Cush is linked to Egypt (Genesis 10:6), the second river, the Gihon (Genesis 2:13), was apparently understood by the author as "the river of Egypt."

Why doesn't the writer simply call the Gihon the "river of Egypt"? The answer lies in his use of historical records. The writer of Genesis shows little desire to edit or modify his historical records. It is likely that these written accounts of the location of the garden of Eden used ancient names which he left intact in his narrative. Such an approach to written sources is common in the biblical narratives (see Genesis 14:7; 28:19; Joshua 15:63).

When we move to Genesis 15, we find that the land promised to Abraham — the promised land — is marked off by these same two rivers, the Euphrates and the River of Egypt (Genesis 15:18). Note that the area marked off by these two rivers in Genesis 15 is essentially the same region covered by the garden of Eden in Genesis 2. When the general boundaries are compared, it becomes clear that the writer of the Pentateuch intends us to identify the two locations with each other. God's promise of the land to the patriarchs is thus textually linked to His original "blessing" of all humanity in the garden of Eden.

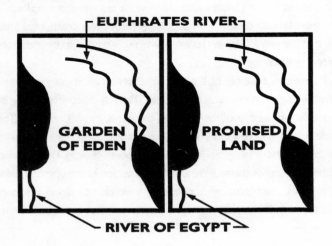

We find the same linkage in the prophetic literature and the New Testament.[4] God's promise of blessing through the seed of Abraham is linked to his blessing of the nations and all humanity.

By establishing a connection between the promised land and the garden of Eden, the Genesis narratives reveal something quite important about God and His purposes in creation. They tell us that God's purposes remain the same. What He has accomplished in creation He will do again in His covenant promises.

Like a loving father, "in the beginning" God gave His children a place to dwell, a good land, filled with divine blessings. So also in His covenant with Israel at Sinai (Exodus 19), God again promised to give them a "good land" where they could enjoy His blessings and have fellowship with Him. They had to remain faithful and obedient, however.

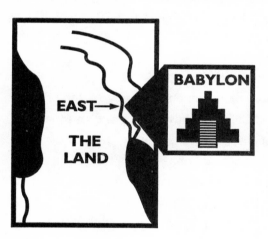

Like Adam and Eve in Genesis 2, Israel can expect to dwell in their "good land" only so long as they are obedient to God's will. When they disobey, God will cast them out of "the land," and they will go "eastward" into Babylon — just as He cast Adam and his family "eastward" out of the garden (Genesis 3:23; 4:16) and into the city of Babylon (Genesis 11:1–9).

We must not forget that the city of Babel built by the descendants of Adam is described in the text as Babylon, "Babel" being the Hebrew name for "Babylon." It was from that city that God called Abraham (Genesis

11:31). Through his "seed" was to come the One who would restore the blessing for all humanity in the promised land (Genesis 12:1–3).

GARDEN AND TABERNACLE

The parallel between the boundaries of the garden of Eden and those of the promised land is not the only important textual link between the creation and the Sinai Covenant. The narrative of the garden of Eden also appears deliberately to foreshadow the description of the tabernacle. The garden, like the tabernacle, was the place where man could enjoy the fellowship and presence of God.

Although we noted earlier that the Pishon and Gihon rivers are difficult to identify, the author's careful description of them can be tied to the parallels between the role of the garden and that of the tabernacle.[5] In describing the garden, the author primarily stresses the beauty of the gold and precious stones throughout the lands encompassed by the garden. Later biblical literature suggests that the purpose of such descriptions is to show the glory of God's presence through the physical beauty of the land.

The prophet Haggai, for example, proclaimed the glory of God's presence in the new temple with a description of the gold and precious metals of that temple: "I will fill this house with glory, says the LORD Almighty. The silver is mine and the gold is mine, declares the LORD Almighty" (Haggai 2:7–8). So also John's description of the New Jerusalem stresses the gold and precious stones which picture the glorious presence of God among His people: "The wall [of the New Jerusalem] was made of jasper, and the city of pure gold, as pure as glass. The foundations of the city walls were decorated with every kind of precious stone" (Revelation 21:18).

In this manner the depiction of the garden foreshadows the tabernacle of God. In light of this, it is especially interesting to find that the description of God's "placing" man in the garden strongly resembles the later establishment of the priesthood for the tabernacle and temple.

After noting that God "put" man into the garden in Genesis 2:8b, the author declares in verse 15 the Lord's purpose in putting him there. Traditional English translations of verse 15 threaten to obscure two important points.

The first is the change in vocabulary for the Hebrew word for "put." Unlike verse 8, where a common term for "put" is used, in verse 15 the author uses a term elsewhere reserved for two special uses:

1. God's "rest" or "safety" which He gives to man in the land (see Genesis 19:16; Deuteronomy 3:20; 12:10; 25:19);

2. The "dedication" of something before the presence of the Lord (see Exodus 16:33–34; Leviticus 16:23; Numbers 17:4; Deuteronomy 26:4, 10).

Both senses of the term appear to lie behind the author's use of the word in verse 15. Man was "put" into the garden where he could "rest" and be "safe;" and man was "put" into the garden "in God's presence" where he could have fellowship with God (3:8).

Second, English translations have often overlooked the specific purpose for God's putting man in the garden. In most versions, man is "put" in the garden "to work it and take care of it" (2:15). Although this interpretation is found in translations as early as the Septuagint, there are serious objections to it. For one, the suffixed pronoun in the Hebrew text (rendered "it" in English) is feminine, whereas the noun "garden" (to which the pronoun refers in English) is masculine. Only by changing the pronoun to a masculine singular, as the Septuagint has done, can it have the sense of the English translations, namely "to work" and "to keep." In the present Hebrew text, the "it" is taken as a reference to "the Law" (ha torah).

A further difficulty in seeing Genesis 2:15 as a reference to man's "working" in the garden is that later in this same narrative, "working the ground" is said to be a result of the Fall (3:23). The narrative thus suggests that the requirement of "work" was an ironic reversal of man's original purpose of "worship." If such is the case, then "working" and "keeping" the garden would provide a poor contrast to "working the ground" after the Fall.

In light of such difficulties, a more suitable translation of the Hebrew text can be found in several early manuscripts: that the man was put into the garden "to worship and obey."[6] Man's life in the garden was to be characterized by worship and obedience. He was to be a priest, not merely a worker and keeper of the garden. Such a reading not only answers the objections raised against the traditional English translation, it also suits the larger ideas of the narrative. Throughout chapter 2, the author has consistently and consciously developed the idea of man's "likeness" to God along the lines of worship and Sabbath rest, the major themes of the Pentateuch.

A further confirmation of the reading "to worship and obey" is that in the following verse (2:16) we read for the first time that "God commanded" (the Hebrew root *tzvh*) the man whom He had created. Just as in the rest of the Torah, enjoyment of God's good land is made contingent on "keeping" God's commandments (see Deuteronomy 30:16, the Hebrew root *tzvh*).

The similarity between this condition for enjoyment of God's blessing and that laid down for Israel at Sinai and in Deuteronomy is clear. One can hear in God's words to the first man Moses' later words to Israel: "See, I set before you today life and blessing [the good, *tob*], death and calamity [the evil, *ra*]. For I am commanding [*tzvh*] you today to love the LORD your God, to walk in his ways, and to keep his commandments, decrees and laws; then you will live and increase, and the LORD your God will bless you in the land [*eretz*] you are entering to possess.... But if your heart turns away and you are not obedient...you will not live long in the land you are crossing the Jordan to enter and possess" (Deuteronomy 30:15–18).

The implication of God's commands in Genesis 2:16–17 and Deuteronomy 30 is that God alone knows what is good (*tob*) for man and God alone knows what is not good (*ra*) for him. To enjoy the good, mankind must trust God and obey Him. If mankind disobeys, he will have to decide for himself what is good and what is not good. While to modern man such a prospect may seem desirable, to the author of Genesis, it is the worst fate imaginable. Only God can know what is good.

IN SUMMARY: THE ROLE OF THE GARDEN

The account of God's preparation of the garden of Eden plays an important role in the larger meaning of Genesis 1 and 2. Central to the account is the concept that the man and woman were created to worship God and obey him. They were made for divine fellowship. The writer of the Pentateuch sees the garden as a kind of early tabernacle within the promised land, a place where God and man could meet. Much attention is thus given to the appearance and location of the garden.

The rivers which run through the garden help the reader situate it within the broader confines of the land promised to Abraham. In this narrative, the garden of Eden represents that lost fellowship between God and human beings — a fellowship which was God's original purpose in creation.

• There are two ways Genesis 1 and 2 can be read. It can be read within the context of the ancient Near Eastern view of the world, or it can be read within the context of the Bible and the world it describes.

• Genesis 1 and 2 are intended to be an introduction to the whole Pentateuch. All the central themes and topics are introduced and given their essential meaning in these first two chapters of Genesis.

• It is essential to read and understand Genesis 1 and 2 within the context of the whole Pentateuch.

CONTEXT IS EVERYTHING

As we have seen, understanding the correct sense of crucial words and phrases is essential to a proper grasp of Genesis 1 and 2. But equally important is gaining a correct view of the *context* in which these words and phrases appear.

How important it is to understand the Bible within the appropriate context! For nearly a millennium Genesis 1 and 2 were read as if they represented the Ptolemaic universe (see Part Four for an extended discussion of this issue). The accuracy of the Bible was made to rest on the validity of the Ptolemaic system. When that system collapsed under pressure from the discoveries of Copernicus, for many people it meant the end of the biblical world view.

Today we see the world from the perspective of modern science and the theories of Albert Einstein. Yet if it was wrong to read the Bible as if it represented the Ptolemaic system, it is equally wrong to read the Bible as if it represents the Einsteinian universe. While the Bible may in fact reflect precisely the modern view of the universe, the evidence should come legitimately from the text; it should not be read into the text from the dictates of science. In other words, the text must be read from a proper context.

But what *is* the appropriate context for reading Genesis 1 and 2? And how is it determined? Today there are at least two possible answers to that question.

Modern historiography has produced and reproduced an enormous amount of literature attempting to reconstruct how the world was viewed in ancient, pre-Western culture. That concept of the world has become known as the ancient Near Eastern view.

According to many modern historians, ancient societies viewed the world in radically different ways than the prevailing Greek culture which so fundamentally influenced the Western world. In the ancient Near Eastern view, the world was not an ordered cosmos which stood in opposition to a disordered chaos.[1] The ancient Near Eastern view of the world was fraught with mythological powers and dark forces. No single "view" of the world dominated, at least in the sense we usually think of it. The world was merely a place where dramas were acted out and the fates of the gods and human beings were determined by their actions. The world was viewed through everyday experiences such as life and death, famine and feast, war and peace.

In the Babylonian account of creation, for example, the world came into existence when the god Marduk drew his sword and cut the ocean goddess Tiamat into two parts. From her remains Marduk fashioned the heavens and upper waters. From the blood of another god, Kingu, Marduk made human beings.[2]

DID THE BIBLE BORROW ITS STORY?

Much debate has focused on the relationship between Genesis 1 and the numerous ancient Near Eastern creation myths. The question has been whether the biblical writer in Genesis 1 borrowed elements of his story from the Babylonian accounts.

That question has been decisively resolved in our day. Most biblical scholars agree that there is little basis for assuming the biblical writer used or had access to any known ancient Near Eastern creation myth.[3]

Another question remains, however — one which has received less attention but in many ways is far more important. Does the Bible share the *general* world view of the ancient Near Eastern creation myths?

Though many have assumed that the Bible shares the world view of the ancient orient, the creation accounts we have from that period are all distinct from the Bible. They are distinctly poetic and manifestly mythological. The biblical account, by contrast, is thoroughly narrative in form and decidedly non-mythological. If we want to understand the relationship between the Bible and the ancient Near Eastern culture in which it was written, we would be wiser to compare the biblical poetic accounts of creation (as in Job 38) with the early ancient Near East accounts.

To compare the narratives of Genesis 1 with the poetic myths of the Babylonians is a classic case of mixing apples and oranges. The primary reason the biblical narratives have been compared with ancient Near Eastern poetry is that no Near Eastern narrative parallels exist. That, in itself, testifies to the distinctive world view of the biblical creation account.

ANCIENT, YES; MYTHOLOGICAL, NO

Though I have not taken the ancient Near Eastern approach in *Genesis Unbound*, I want to acknowledge its strengths and essential validity. The Bible *is* an ancient book, written to people in an ancient world, with a quite different outlook than ours. We will miss the message and meaning of the Bible if we foist our viewpoint and perspectives on the writers.

Therefore, to ensure that we treat the text appropriately, we must identify its proper context. Fortunately, that is possible.

PRESENT LITERARY CONTEXT

A second way we can seek to discover the appropriate context for understanding Genesis 1 and 2 — and I believe the correct way — is to view them in their literary context. The first two chapters of Genesis were not meant to be read in isolation from the rest of the Pentateuch (Genesis, Exodus, Leviticus, Numbers, Deuteronomy). These two chapters present a general description of the world in which the subsequent historical events will take place. They set the stage.

The creation account in Genesis 1 and 2 shows great selectivity and design. It is precisely that selectivity we should seek to understand, because the design of the text should point to the meaning the author intended to convey.

In reading Genesis 1 and 2, therefore, we need to ask several questions: What is the overall purpose of the Pentateuch? What is its central theme? In what way do Genesis 1 and 2 help us understand that theme? How do these early chapters prepare us for understanding and appreciating all that follows in the Pentateuch?

When viewed within the literary context of the whole Pentateuch, the Genesis account of creation not only makes good sense but also fits well with current and long-standing scientific views of the world.

GENESIS 1 WITHIN THE CONTEXT OF THE PENTATEUCH

Genesis 1 is often read as if it were merely an account of God's creation of the universe. It is that, of course, but it is much more. The opening verse clearly states that God created all things. But throughout the rest of the chapter, the narrative focuses on God's preparation of "the land." *The primary purpose of Genesis 1 is to show that God made "the land" and prepared it as a place for the man and woman to dwell in peace.*

The events recorded in Genesis 1 have been carefully selected and arranged to serve a unique role as an introduction to the whole of the Pentateuch. The story recounted in these early chapters is thus both theological and historical in nature. It tells us the way things were, and it attempts to tell us something about the will of God for our lives.

In Genesis 1 the author carefully sets the stage for the narratives which follow: the primeval history (chapters 2–11) and the patriarchs (chapters 12–50). Also in these early narratives the author provides the necessary background for understanding the central topic of the Pentateuch: God's covenant with Israel at Mount Sinai. In nearly every sentence of the creation account the author's interests in the Sinai Covenant and God's chosen people can be clearly seen. There is much which deals with God's purpose for all humanity as well.

In the Sinai Covenant, God entered a relationship with Israel in which He promised to be their God and make them His people. He vowed to give them the "land" He had promised to their forefathers. He promised to bless them in that land, to give them rest and peace, and ultimately to dwell with them in that land. Thus the concept of the "land" is central to the purpose of the Pentateuch and the Sinai Covenant. It was God's ultimate goal to bless His people in the promised land.

In the Sinai Covenant, God also called on Israel to obey Him. In fact, that was the only condition God placed on their enjoyment of the land. If they disobeyed, Israel would be cast out of the land and go into exile (Deuteronomy 4:25–26).

Each of these central themes of the Sinai Covenant finds its initial statement in the opening chapters of Genesis. The Covenant is grounded in the events of creation. The author of Genesis 1 wants to show that the stretch of land which God promised to give Israel in the Sinai Covenant — the land where Abraham and his family sojourned, the land of Canaan — was the same land God had prepared for them at the time of creation. It was in *that* land that God first blessed mankind and called upon men and women to obey him. In was in *that* land that the Tree of Life once grew and God provided for man's good and kept him from evil. In the narrative of Genesis 1, we are thus given an account of God's original purposes with humanity.

CREATION AND COVENANT

The theological perspective of this first section of Genesis can be summarized in two points.

First, the author intends to draw a line connecting the God of the fathers and of the Sinai Covenant with the God who created the world. That is the purpose of the very first verse in the Bible: "In the beginning God created the heavens and the earth." The God spoken of here is the God of the Sinai Covenant. The Bible thus begins with the statement that the Covenant God created the universe.

Second, the author wants to show that the Sinai Covenant and God's call of Abraham have as their ultimate goal the establishment of God's original purposes in creation. God intended from the beginning that His people find blessing and peace in "the land" He provided for them.

In Genesis 1 and 2, God created a place for the man and the woman to dwell — the "land." There, in "the land," they were to enjoy His blessing (Genesis 1:28). There we see God's people living in peace and enjoying God's blessing.

These two themes dominate the portrayal of creation in Genesis 1. They are also closely related. God's blessing is to be found in the land which He created.

From the beginning of the creation account, God's interest in the land lies at center stage. After establishing the larger point that God created the universe (Genesis 1:1), the writer turns immediately to give an account of God's preparation of the land (1:2). Thus it is that the remainder of the creation account (1:2–2:4a) is devoted to the narrative record of God's preparation of the land.

This land continues to occupy the attention of the writer throughout Genesis. We learn that it was this land which mankind abandoned, moving eastward where the city of Babylon was built (11:1–9). It was out of Babylon that God called Abraham. Abraham was to leave Babylon and return to the land which God promised to him and his descendants (15:18). It was in this land that God had promised to bless Abraham, and it is in this land that all the nations will be blessed along with the descendants of Abraham (12:3). This is a constant and recurring image in Scripture.

When the land and the blessing were lost as a result of the Fall, the biblical narratives take up the story of God's restoration of mankind and the land (Genesis 4–Deuteronomy 34). In those narratives we see that God restored mankind and the land through His covenants. He made a covenant with Noah (Genesis 9); then with Abraham (Genesis 15); and then again with the people of Israel (Exodus 19). The latter covenant was renewed on the borders of the promised land in the last chapters of the Pentateuch (Deuteronomy 5–30).

The biblical covenants are thus marked off in the Pentateuch as God's means of restoring His lost creation. In fact, the whole of biblical revelation points to a time when God will restore creation to that original purpose (cf. Revelation 21:1–4).

Thus creation and covenant, or creation and redemption, are the central themes of the Pentateuch. One aspect of God's dealings with the world — creation — cannot be fully understood without the other — the covenant.

IN SUMMARY: AN ESSENTIAL PREREQUISITE

By paying close attention to the details of Genesis 1, we can understand a great deal about the author's purpose in writing the Pentateuch. In the details he selects to write about, we find the clues to his focus.

Yet if we wish to fully understand Genesis 1, we must not focus exclusively on the details but rather begin within the broader framework of the Pentateuch. Such a perspective is an essential prerequisite for understanding this passage.

With that in mind, we are almost ready to consider a fresh exposition of Genesis 1 and 2. But before we do, let's put together some of the details we've just looked at and fit them into a coherent picture. Then we'll be ready to tackle the richness of the biblical text itself.

• We should read Genesis 1 in terms of its connections to Genesis 2.

• By reading Genesis 1 and 2 together we can identify the "land" in Genesis 1 as the garden of Eden in Genesis 2.

• The first verse in Genesis 1 is not limited to the "land." It asserts that God created the whole universe. The writer focuses on the "promised land" in the verses which follow, Genesis 1:2–2:25.

• To say that the creation account focuses on the promised land doesn't mean that it lacks universal implications. God's concern has always been for the whole world. The biblical message is that God's work of redemption is centered in His work in the promised land.

• The week in Genesis 1 is a literal, seven-day week. The days are literal, twenty-four-hour days.

• God's work and rest during this week is presented as a picture of mankind's work and rest.

CHAPTER EIGHT

THE LAND AND THE BLESSING

Two themes are especially important to the author of Genesis. Throughout the first two chapters of Genesis and the whole Pentateuch, Moses keeps coming back to the preparation of the land and the divine blessing. These key themes form the basis of his treatment of the patriarchal narratives and the Sinai Covenant.

If we look carefully, we see that the first two chapters of Genesis form a single unit with three primary sections. The first section consists of verse 1, which stands apart from the rest of the chapter; section two consists of 1:2–2:3, God's preparation of the land; and 2:4b–25 tells the story of God's preparation of the garden of Eden. The heading in 2:4a, "generations," connects these last two sections. In recounting the events of creation, the author has selected and arranged his narrative so that the two themes are allowed full development.

A HOMELAND FOR GOD'S PEOPLE

The writer of the Pentateuch wrote Genesis 1 primarily because he wanted his readers to understand something about God and the nature of the covenant He made with Israel at Mt. Sinai. At the center of that covenant was the promise of a homeland for His people (Deuteronomy 5:32–33). Already in the first chapter of the Pentateuch the author directs the readers to God's concern for that land.[1]

Thus, the theme of the Sinai Covenant — God's good gift of the promised land — lies at the center of the author's account of creation. In the covenant, God promised Israel that if they would obey Him and keep His covenant, He would give them the good land promised their forefathers. In creation, God's purposes were precisely the same. The first man and woman were to obey God's command and enjoy His good land forever (Genesis 2:16–17).

God began His work of preparing the "land" for Israel by first bringing the morning sunlight, by separating the waters from the dry land, and by furnishing the land with its rich resources for man's nourishment (1:2–27).

Having prepared the land and its resources, God then gave them to the first man and woman. It was to be their "land" to enjoy. That was the plan of the divine blessing. There, in the land, they were to "be fruitful, multiply" and to fill the land (Genesis 1:28). Yet mankind's enjoyment of the land was conditional upon their obedience to God's will (2:16f). As long as they obeyed God and kept His commandments, they could enjoy His "good land" forever. If they disobeyed God, however, they would be cast off the land and they would die.

Those, of course, were the same conditions under which Israel herself was to enjoy that very same land. If they obeyed God and kept His commandments, they would live long in that land (Deuteronomy 30:16–20). If they disobeyed, they would be cast off the land and taken into exile (Deuteronomy 4:25–26).

GENESIS I AND THE GARDEN OF EDEN

One especially puzzling question about Genesis 1 and 2 has troubled biblical expositors for centuries. What is the relationship between the account of creation in Genesis 1 and the account of God's preparing the garden of Eden in Genesis 2? Are these two distinct accounts of creation? Do they reflect two different sources used by the writer of the Pentateuch? Or is one account a further elaboration or explanation of the other?

Many modern scholars believe there is no inherent relationship between the two accounts. They hold that these two accounts represent different and contradictory narratives of creation.

For example, in Genesis 1 it appears that God makes the whole world in six days and rests on the seventh day. He makes the sun, moon, and stars, and all the animals on earth. The scope and focus of the first account seems to be the whole universe. In Genesis 2, God is concerned only with the garden of Eden. There is no mention of His making the rest of the universe. He merely makes the man and woman and a few animals, which He brings to the man to name. In Genesis 1, God makes the animals before He makes the man and woman; in Genesis 2, God makes the animals after He makes man, but before He makes the woman.

Some English translations have obscured the difference between these two accounts by translating Genesis 2:19 with the English perfect tense: "Now the Lord God *had formed* out of the ground all the beasts of the field and all the birds of the air." When the English text says God "had formed" the animals, it implies the animals were made before the man was created, just as Genesis 1 indicates. The problem, however, is that the Hebrew text doesn't contain the proper verb form for such a translation. In chapter 2 the clear meaning of the Hebrew verb is that the animals were created (2:19) *after* the man (2:7) and *before* the woman (2:22). Thus the scope and focus of the second account is only the garden of Eden.

The view which sees the two creation accounts in Genesis 1 and 2 as contradictory has come under increasing scrutiny in recent years, even by those who have no real interest in whether there are contradictions and errors in Scripture. Many modern biblical scholars believe it is unrealistic to suppose that the original author of the Pentateuch would have been unaware of such possible contradictions between the two chapters. It is more likely that the author was well aware of the differences between the two accounts yet did not see those differences as contradictory, but rather as part of the overall meaning of the two chapters.

The author of Genesis and the Pentateuch expected his readers to understand his work as a unit. By attaching these two different and distinct accounts of creation in Genesis 1 and 2, he expected his readers to see a meaningful link between them. God's creation of the man and woman in Genesis 2 was intended to give the reader another view of God's creation of humanity in Genesis 1. The narrative events in Genesis 2 were to be understood by the reader as a broader perspective on the events of Genesis 1. The differences between the two accounts were precisely what the author wanted his readers to be aware of. Those differences broaden our understanding of the narrative events.

Judging from the way these two narratives have been read in the past, the author was apparently successful in his purpose. Traditionally, these two narratives have most commonly been read as complementary to each other. Chapter 2 has been understood as a more detailed account of the events of the sixth day when God made the man and woman. The idea that the two narratives present distinct and contradictory accounts is more a statement about the viewpoint of modern readers than the intention of the ancient writer.

If, then, we are to understand Genesis 1 within the context of the whole of the Pentateuch, we must say something about its relationship to the account of God's preparation of the garden of Eden in Genesis 2. What does the story of God's preparing the garden of Eden tell us about the events in Genesis 1?

SEEING THE LINKS

If the creation account in Genesis 1 is related to the record of God's preparing the garden of Eden, then, to some extent or in some way, Genesis 1 must be about the garden of Eden. Though much of the classical discussions of Genesis 1 and 2 have tacitly acknowledged this relationship between the two accounts, rarely has it been explicitly drawn into the interpretation of chapter 1. The implication is that the account of the creation of the "land" in Genesis 1 is actually about the garden of Eden.

Just how far should we take that connection? Just how much of the story in Genesis 2 are we to read back into our understanding of Genesis 1?

The relationship between Genesis 1 and 2 follows a common pattern seen throughout the further narratives of the primeval history (Genesis 1–11). The author often links two distinct narratives to reflect a specific textual strategy. For example, after a narrative with a general description of an event, the author often attaches one which gives more detail about the same event. Having described the dispersion of the nations "according to their languages and countries" in Genesis 10, the author attaches the story of the city of Babylon (Tower of Babel) in Genesis 11:1–9 to explain the origin of their different languages.

In a similar way, in Genesis 1 we are given a general description of God's work of creation. In Genesis 2 we see a "close-up" of certain aspects of the account in Genesis 1. We see, in fact, the preparation of the garden of Eden and the creation of the man and woman in that garden.

There are important implications of such narrative links. One particular linkage deserves special consideration — the identification of the "land" and the garden of Eden. The link between Genesis 1 and 2 casts considerable light on the author's purpose in these creation accounts. If chapters 1 and 2 recount the same event, then the "land" where the garden of Eden is located in chapter 2 is identified with the "land" which God makes in chapter 1. Moreover if the "land" where the garden of Eden is located is the promised land of the patriarchal narratives, then the focus of the creation account is that same "land." If I am right, then Genesis 1 is an account of God's preparation of the promised land. One can easily see how a later writer such as Jeremiah would have drawn the conclusion that Genesis 1 was specifically about God's preparation of the promised land (see Jeremiah 27:5).

THE CREATOR

The focus or scope of Genesis 1:1 is the account of divine creation. It proclaims God's creation of the universe and tells us that the universe is not eternal. Only God is eternal; all else was created by Him. God created the universe "out of nothing." There is hardly a verse in the Bible that carries as much weight as Genesis 1:1. The whole of the Bible's view of God rests on that single, initial statement.

However, the viewpoint of the writer shifts considerably in the second verse. In the rest of Genesis 1 and 2, the writer no longer focuses on God's creation of the universe but on the promised land, Israel's homeland. As he writes the whole of this account, the author wants us to think both about God's creation of the universe and about the promised land.

The writer wants us to see God as both the Creator of the universe and the One who prepares a land for His people. That is one of the central themes of the Pentateuch. If we keep that perspective in mind, we will see a surprising and remarkable picture of creation unfold from the narratives of Genesis 1 and 2. We will see a remarkable picture of the Creator emerge, as well.

In these early chapters of the Bible, we do not find a distant, detached Creator at work on far-flung worlds. We do not find a God who is off, busy in some other galaxy. God has made the heavens and the other galaxies, but we find Him at work in our own world in Genesis 1. We find Him as a loving Father, carefully and thoughtfully preparing a specific place for His children to dwell. He creates a world for them and then prepares a place, a homeland, for them in His world.

Thus the Pentateuch teaches that when Israel was promised a land in which to live out God's blessings (Genesis 15:18), it was not the first time God had prepared a place for them. From the beginning, God had prepared that place for His chosen people. When He took it away from the Canaanites and gave it to His people, He did so because they had abused their right to live in His land (Genesis 15:16). In the same way, if the Israelites were to abuse their right to live in God's land, He would also take the land away from them and give it to another (Jeremiah 27:1–6). The land was God's gift. It was His land; He created it, and He could give it to whomever He pleased (Jeremiah 27:5).

The concept of the "land" thus dominates the whole of the theology of the Pentateuch. The early narratives of Genesis already prepare the reader for God's great promise to the fathers, the gift of the promised land.

A GLOBAL PERSPECTIVE

In focusing on the "land," I don't mean that God didn't create the rest of the earth or that the biblical writer was unconcerned about the rest of the earth. On the contrary, one of the central points of the Genesis creation account is God's concern for the whole world shown by the blessing that will come to this "land." The "land" is the stage for God's plan of blessing. In this very land God will bless not only His own people, Israel, but all the nations of the earth.

It is already clear within the Pentateuch that the messianic King will one day come to this land. He will arise from the tribe of Judah (Genesis 49:8–12) and establish His kingdom in this land (Numbers 24:5–9, 16–24). He, like Melchizedek, the king of Jerusalem, will bless Abraham and his seed in this land (Genesis 14:18–20), and through Him, all the families of the earth will be blessed (Genesis 12:3). The fact that the account of creation focuses on the promised land in no way limits its

---

THEISTIC EVOLUTION

According to most versions of theistic evolution, God created the universe and all life using the process of evolution and natural selection. The biblical account of creation is a picturesque way to say that God was behind evolution and the geological formation of the earth. Genesis 1 should not be taken literally; it tells us that God created the world, but it does not tell us how He did it. We know how God created the world from the facts of science.

Theistic evolutionists, like creationists, view the meaning of the biblical account in terms of their scientific understanding of the world. Evolution was the means by which God created the world. In this way the meaning of Genesis 1 is "explained" by scientific laws and theory. Theistic evolutionists attempt to show that the Bible is "true," albeit in a figurative sense. They do not see Genesis 1 in realistic and literal terms and often scorn attempts to do so, labeling them as obscurantism.

---

universal scope. It only limits its perspective, and to understand it correctly we must read it from that perspective.

We must not forget that in the first verse of the chapter the writer tells us quite clearly that God created the universe — "the heavens and earth." That expression includes the sun, moon, stars, and all the earth. God's creation of the universe is thus an important part of the meaning of Genesis 1. Yet from the perspective of the Pentateuch as a whole, this forms merely the introduction to the central theme of God's preparation of the promised land. The God of creation is the God of the covenant. He is the God who has created the universe; He is also the God who has provided a good land for His people and who cares for them as a loving Father.

As long as Adam and Eve serve God and keep His commandments, God will continue to provide them with blessings and the good provisions they need. Their ultimate destiny is to live forever, at rest, in this good land. To that end God has put a tree of life in the midst of the garden. If Adam and Eve obey God, they can enjoy God's gift of the land forever.

It doesn't take much imagination to see that the themes of these early chapters of Genesis are precisely those of the remainder of the Pentateuch. The warning given the first man and woman is precisely the warning given to Israel at Sinai and throughout the remainder of the Pentateuch. If Israel served God and kept His commandments, God would provide them with all their needs. They would dwell peacefully, at rest, in the land.

When, in the course of the early Genesis narratives, the man and the woman disobey God, they are cast out of the garden. The author tells us specifically that when they left the land, the man and his wife were sent "eastward." In the Pentateuch, "eastward" is the location of the city of Babylon (Genesis 11:2). Just as a rebellious Israel was later sent into Babylonian captivity, Adam and Eve, God's first chosen people, were also sent "eastward" and hence away from God's presence. Moreover, a great catastrophe awaited them in which the whole of God's creation was destroyed in the flood. Yet in the midst of those signs of judgment, God

had made a promise of redemption. There was hope for the future —
although as the narratives unfold, there seems to be little else.

The alert reader of these narratives begins to see that throughout the
remaining chapters of Genesis, God's promise of redemption takes on central importance. By means of a promised redeemer God's original purposes for humanity in the garden of Eden would be accomplished again in
the promised land. Creation and redemption are thus the two great
themes of the Pentateuch and the whole of the Bible. Both themes are
grounded in the events recorded in these early chapters of Genesis.

A SINGLE WEEK

God's preparation of the promised land extended over a single week. That
week, as far as we can gather from the text itself, was a normal week of six
twenty-four-hour days and a seventh day in which God rested. Why did
God take six days to do a work that He could have done in a single
moment? The answer to that question lies in the larger purpose of the
writer of the Pentateuch.

In Exodus 20:11, in the midst of His instruction on keeping the seventh day as a day of rest, God himself alluded to this very account of
preparing the "sky, the land, and the sea." That work, God said, took six
days and was followed by a day of rest. In working six days and resting on
the seventh, God established a pattern for mankind's own work and rest.
Just as God worked six days, so also man was to work six days. Just as God
rested on the seventh day and called it holy, so man was to rest on the seventh day and treat it as holy.

As the biblical writer thus put it, God deliberately worked for six full
days to provide an example for mankind's labors. The picture we see of
God in these chapters is a father setting an example for his children. The
prophet Hosea alluded to this when he said God "taught them to walk by
leading them in his own footsteps" (Hosea 11:3).

That is the kind of God the writer of Genesis introduces us to. He is
not distant and aloof but close by and deeply caring. Because of His great

love, He prepared a land for His people, a delightful place for their habitation. He carefully designed the land for them so they would be able to thrive there, and He called all of it into being merely by speaking His word. It is an awesome picture, and one well worth deeper investigation.

PART THREE

GENESIS UNBOUND

CHAPTER NINE

GOD AT THE CENTER

GENESIS 1:1

For the sake of clarity, the purpose of this third part of *Genesis Unbound* is to give a simple, straightforward exposition of the main points I think the author is making in Genesis 1 and 2. I will clarify why I hold my views and, as needed, will discuss the more technical aspects in the footnotes. My chief goal is hermeneutical — What does the biblical text say about creation?

Before I present my exposition, however, I offer an "interpretive translation" of Genesis 1:1–2:4a. In this way we can get our bearings as we strike out on what I hope is an accurate explanation of the biblical creation account — an explanation rooted in the text itself which solves most of the interpretive problems noted for centuries by careful Bible students.

AN INTERPRETIVE TRANSLATION OF GENESIS 1:1–2:4A

[1] Long ago God created the world. He created the sun, the moon, and the stars, as well as all the creatures which inhabit the earth. He created all of them out of nothing — not in a single instant of time, but over a vast period of time.

[2] God's world, however, was not complete. He had not yet created human beings and the land where he intended to put them was not yet suitable for them. It was covered by a deep ocean and the sun could not penetrate the dense fog which covered the waters. God's Spirit, however, was already present over

the waters covering the land. ³ One day God set out to prepare the land for human beings. First, while the darkness of night still hung over the vast surface of the waters, God spoke, calling on the sun to rise and break through the dense fog. At His command, the daylight broke through the darkness. ⁴ God saw that, now, the land was on its way to becoming a very good place for the man and woman to dwell. ⁵ God named the sunlight "day," and the darkness He named "night." When the sun broke through the darkness that morning, it showed that a special work of God had begun.

⁶ On the second day of that week, God again spoke. This time He commanded the fog to lift up from upon the waters to form clouds over the land. ⁷ In that way God filled the sky over the land with clouds. ⁸ He also named the area where the clouds floated overhead, the "skies."

⁹ On the third day of that week, God spoke again, commanding the waters upon the land to gather into lakes, rivers, and streams so that there would be dry land for human beings and water for the beautiful garden He was preparing for them. ¹⁰ When they had obeyed His command, He named the dry areas the "land," and the lakes, rivers, and streams where the waters now gathered He named the "seas." God saw that the dry land was now good for human beings. ¹¹ On that same day, God spoke a second time, commanding the land to sprout fruit trees. ¹² The land obeyed and was immediately covered with trees bearing all sorts of fruit. This too God saw was good for human beings. ¹³ That was the end of the third day.

¹⁴ As He had done on each of the preceding days, God spoke on the fourth day to issue a decree that the heavenly bodies were to serve a particular purpose for those who were to dwell on the land. They were to remind God's creatures of His power and grace, and they were to mark the arrival of the great feast days

when His people were to worship Him in the land. [15] Such special purposes for the heavenly bodies were in addition to their natural function as sources of light upon the land. [16] So we see that God had a purpose in mind when long ago He created the sun and the moon, as well as the stars. They were to provide a time frame for those who dwell on the land. [17] God also put them in the sky to provide bright light in the daytime [18] and faint light in the night — this was good for human beings. [19] So ended the fourth day.

[20] On the fifth day, God spoke again. He commanded the fish and water creatures to fill the lakes, rivers, and streams in the land and the birds to fill the skies over the land. [21] On that same day God created sea creatures and birds of all sizes to dwell in the land. [22] Moreover, God blessed them so that they might abundantly increase throughout the land and skies. [23] That was the end of the events of the fifth day.

[24] Once more God spoke. This time on the beginning of the sixth day, He commanded the land to bring forth various kinds of animal life: small creatures, domesticated creatures, and wild animals. [25] So it was God who made those creatures for the land. These, He saw, would be good for man.

[26] On that same day, God spoke again. He said, "Let us make human beings. Let us make them persons like ourselves. And let them rule over all the other creatures in the land, those in the skies, the seas, and the dry land." [27] So God created human beings. He made them persons — male and female. [28] Then He spoke once again. This time He blessed the human beings with the promise of having children and families in the land He had just prepared for them. [29] Then, for the tenth and last time, God spoke again. "See all the fruit trees I have made in this land," He said. "I put them there for your nourishment. [30] Also, the animals may eat the other vegetation which will grow in the land." [31] Finally, God

saw that all He had made in the land was very good for the man and the woman.

²:¹ The world which God had made was now complete. ² So, on the seventh day, God ceased working. ³ He blessed and sanctified the seventh day as the time to cease from one's work and worship God. ⁴ᵃ That is the story of the creation of the world.

A TITLE?

The Genesis creation account opens with a simple and concise statement: "In the beginning God created the heavens and the earth" (Genesis 1:1). A more precise translation would be "In the beginning God created the sky and the land."

In recent years it has become commonplace to take this first verse as a title for the whole chapter. Verse 1 tells us that the whole chapter is about God's creating "the heavens and the earth." The sense of the verse would thus be "In the beginning, God created the heavens and the earth. Now this is how it happened. The earth was empty and void and darkness was upon the face of the deep, and God said, 'Let there be light'...."

But is this correct? Can we think of Genesis 1:1 as a title? I believe there are at least three reasons why such an interpretation is not likely. Two are technical, while the third follows the lines of common sense.

THREE OBJECTIONS

1. *In the original the first verse is a complete sentence that makes a statement, but titles are not formed that way in Hebrew.*

In Hebrew, titles consist of simple phrases.[1] If Genesis 1:1 were a title, we would expect it to say something like, "God's creation of the heavens and earth," or at least, "This is an account of God's creating the heavens and the earth."

We can compare Genesis 1:1 with Genesis 5:1 ("This is the book of the genealogy of Adam"), which clearly serves as a title for the rest of chapter 5. Closer to home is the title in Genesis 2:4a: "This is the genealogy of the heavens and the earth when they were created." This also is quite different from the sentence in Genesis 1:1. It's so different because 2:4a intends to serve as a title, while 1:1 does not.

2. *The conjunction "and" at the beginning of the second verse makes it highly unlikely that 1:1 is a title.*

This is perhaps the most telling argument against understanding Genesis 1:1 as a title or summary of the first chapter. Though it might seem like a minor point, Hebrew grammar uses this conjunction carefully. If verse 1 were a title, the section immediately following it would surely not begin with the conjunction "and."[2]

3. *Genesis 1 has a summary title at its conclusion, making it unlikely it would have another at its beginning.*

As would be expected, the closing summary comes in the form of a statement: "Thus the heavens and earth were finished, and all their hosts" (Genesis 2:1). Such a clear summary statement *at the close of the narrative* suggests that 1:1 has a purpose other than serving as a title or summary. We would not expect two summaries for one chapter.

For all these reasons, we may take it as virtually certain that the older interpretation of 1:1 is correct: The verse describes God's first work of creating the world. The first verse tells us what God did "in the beginning." He "created the heavens and the earth." The rest of the chapter goes on to describe the further work of God subsequent to that creation. In other words, the rest of the chapter is *not* an elaboration of Genesis 1:1; rather, it is an account of a different and subsequent act of God.

THE NARRATIVE PURPOSE OF GENESIS 1:1

If Genesis 1:1 is not a title, what is its purpose? The purpose of the opening statement in Genesis is twofold: It identifies the Creator; and it explains the origin of the world.

1. *The Identity of the Creator*

The Creator is identified in 1:1 as the biblical God (*Elohim*). It is important to note that God is not further identified in the first verse, as He sometimes is elsewhere in the Pentateuch. In Genesis 15:7, for example, God says to Abraham, "I am the God *who brought you out of Ur of the Chaldeans.*" In Exodus 20:2 God says, "I am the God *who brought you out of the land of Egypt.*" It is enough in Genesis 1:1 simply to say that the Creator of the world is God, the biblical God. The author appears confident that there will be no mistaking this God with any other God than the God of the fathers and the God of the covenant at Sinai.

From the start, therefore, we see that the proper context for understanding 1:1 is the whole of the Book of Genesis and the Pentateuch. The work of creation is the work of the Covenant God. A little later (Genesis 2:4b) God is identified with the LORD, Yahweh, the God who called Abraham (Genesis 12:1) and delivered Israel from Egypt (Exodus 3:15). The God of Genesis 1:1 is later identified specifically as the God who called the fathers into His good land, redeemed them from Egypt, and led His people again to the borders of the land, a land which He provided and now called upon them to enter and possess.

By identifying the God of the covenant with the Creator of the universe, a crucial distinction is introduced between the God of the fathers and the gods of the nations, which to the biblical authors were mere idols. The author's point is that God alone created the heavens and earth. The sense of 1:1 is similar to that message which Israel was to carry to all the nations: "Tell them this," Jeremiah said. "'These gods, who did not make the heavens and the earth, will perish from the earth and from under the heavens'" (Jeremiah 10:11). Psalm 96:5 also shows that the purpose of Genesis 1:1 was fully appreciated by later biblical writers: "For all the gods of the nations are idols, but the LORD [Yahweh] made the heavens." God's work of creation is always the Bible's final ground of appeal in establishing God's power and deity.

2. *The Origin of the World*

The statement in 1:1 not only identifies the Creator, it also explains the origin of the world. According to the natural sense of 1:1, God created all that exists in the universe. As it stands, the statement affirms that

God alone is eternal and that all else owes its origin and existence to Him.

The influence of this verse is reflected throughout the work of later biblical writers (see Psalm 33:6; John 1:3; Hebrews 11:3). According to Genesis 1:1, creation had a beginning, but God does not. If Genesis 1:1 says that God created all that exists "in the beginning," then before the "beginning" nothing must have existed.

THE MEANING OF GENESIS 1:1

We turn now to a discussion of the meaning of the first verse in the Bible, looking at each part of this important verse. In the original Hebrew text there are only seven words in the verse. That fits a larger numerical pattern throughout this chapter and the remainder of the Pentateuch.[3]

The first word, *bereshit*, translated "in the beginning," tells us that God created the universe over a period of time, not in a single instance. The length of that period of time is not specified. It could have been as long as billions of years or as short as a few days or years. Given what appears to be true about the age of the earth, it is likely that millions or billions of years transpired during this time of "the beginning." When my children ask me where the dinosaurs fit into the biblical account of creation, I tell them they were created, lived, and became extinct during "the beginning."

The next two words, "God created," tell us that the universe is not eternal. It has a Creator, which implies that the universe was created "out of nothing." While we would be hard pressed to prove that idea from the use of the Hebrew word "created" in this verse — there is no single word in biblical Hebrew which expresses exactly that idea — we can say that the word used to express the idea of God's creating the world was deliberately chosen to give this text a sense of a special act of God, one in which something entirely new was created and which God alone was capable of doing.

The last four words in the Hebrew text of this verse, "the heavens and the earth," are the biblical author's way of describing the entire universe. If we are to understand this expression in the same sense it has throughout

Scripture, then it must refer to the whole of the universe as we know it today. It includes not only the earth, but the sun, moon, and stars. It also includes all that we see around us — plants, animals, rocks, rivers, mountains — you name it. They were all created during a period of time which this verse calls "the beginning." Were it not for the rest of Genesis, particularly the genealogies in chapters 5 and 10, we would be correct to include human beings among the creatures which inhabited the earth at that time. The genealogies in Genesis, however, tell us clearly that all human beings on earth are descendants of the man and woman created on the sixth day of the week which follows. We are thus forced by the logic of the text to exclude humans from the world created "in the beginning."

A POSSIBLE OBJECTION

The mention of God's "making" (*asah*) the "heavens and earth" in six days (Exodus 20:11) may suggest to some readers that the Exodus passage understands Genesis 1 to say that God "created the universe" in six days. If so, wouldn't that contradict what I have said about the meaning of Genesis 1:2–2:4?

The answer to that question lies in the distinction between what Exodus 20:11 *appears* to say and what it actually *says*. Exodus 20:11 does *not* say God "made the heavens and earth" in six days. It says, rather, that God "made the heavens and the earth, the sea, and all that is in *them*" in six days.

In other words, this passage in Exodus does not use the merism "heavens and earth" to describe God's work of six days. Rather, it gives us a list of God's distinct works during the six days. According to that list, God made "the heavens, and the earth, the sea, and all that is in them" in six days. That list refers to God's work in Genesis 1:2–2:4, *not* to His creation of the universe in Genesis 1:1. Exodus 20:11 does not say God *created* "the heavens and earth" in six days; it says God *made* three things in six days — the sky, the land, and the seas — and then filled them during that same period.

It is important to note that in Genesis 1:2–2:4 we are told specifically that God made just these three things. First God "made" the "expanse" and called it the "sky" (Genesis 1:6–8). He then caused the dry land to appear and called it the "land" (Genesis 1:9–10). At that time also He made the "pools of water" in the land and called them "seas." That was during the first three days. In the remainder of the six days of that week, God filled the sky, land, and seas with life.

Exodus 20:11 is thus not speaking of Genesis 1:1, where God "created" the universe, but Genesis 1:2–2:4, where God "made" the sky, land, and seas, and then filled them. By the same token, later references to these events in the Pentateuch (for example, Exodus 31:17) are most likely to be understood as abbreviated forms of this same expression. Hence, like Exodus 20:11, they are not speaking of Genesis 1:1, but of Genesis 1:2–2:4b.

This brings up another question. Why does God have to "make" the sky, land, and seas during the following week if He has already created them "in the beginning"?

We must be careful to observe how the biblical writer uses such terms as "to make" and "to create." In Genesis 1:1, the writer tells us God "created" the universe. In Exodus 20:11, the same writer tells us that God "made" the sky, land, and seas. Surely when God "created" the universe, it included the sky, land, and seas. Certainly there was a physical sky over the land. On the second day when God separated the waters which covered the land, he did not "create" the sky and land. They were already there.

When the text says that on the second day God "made" the sky and the land, it means the same as the English expression "to make" a bed. Elsewhere in the Bible the same Hebrew word is used to describe cutting one's fingernails (Deuteronomy 21:12), washing one's feet (2 Samuel 19:25), and trimming one's beard (2 Samuel 19:24). The same word also means "to appoint" and "to acquire." The word means to put something in good order, to make it right. When the land was covered with water, it was not yet right (or fit) for human beings. God commanded the waters to recede from the land so that it would be a dry place for human habitation. It was in that sense that God "made" the land and the sky on the second day.

A parallel to this idea appears at the conclusion of the flood account in Genesis 9. There we are told that God put a rainbow in the sky as a reminder of his covenant promise to Noah (Genesis 9:13, 16). That does not imply there had never been a rainbow before that time; the rainbow, a result of the nature of light created "in the beginning," had always been in the clouds. The writer tells us in Genesis 9:13 that, from that point on, rainbows were to be God's reminder of His promise.

In the same way, ever since "the beginning," there had been a sky and a land. When God "fixed" the sky and land on the second and third day of the week in Genesis 1:2–2:2a, He did so in behalf of the man and woman He was about to create on the sixth day.

CHAPTER TEN

THE FIRST DAY

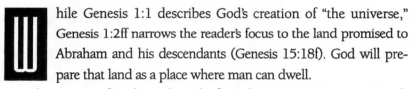

hile Genesis 1:1 describes God's creation of "the universe," Genesis 1:2ff narrows the reader's focus to the land promised to Abraham and his descendants (Genesis 15:18f). God will prepare that land as a place where man can dwell.

The account of God's work on the first[1] day opens in Genesis 1:2 with a description of the "land" before God prepared it for human beings. Again, the term "land" should not be understood as the whole earth but as the promised land. It was the place where the first man and woman were to dwell after they were created. It was ultimately the land promised to the patriarchs Abraham, Isaac, and Jacob, and their descendants, the people of Israel. It was the land where, on some future day, all the nations would again gather to worship God and pay homage to His King, the Messiah (Isaiah 2:1–4; cf. 66:18–24). In this way the beginning and end of the Bible look to precisely the same stretch of land.

SETTING THE STAGE

Genesis 1:2 plays a central role in the writer's overall purpose in Genesis 1. Genesis 1:2 sets the stage for the account of God's actions in the remainder of the chapter. It turns the reader's attention away from the universe as a whole and onto the promised land, which is the central setting of the remainder of the Pentateuch.

Genesis 1:2 describes the condition of the promised land before God began to prepare it as a place for Adam and Eve to dwell. It was not yet inhabitable, nor was it a place of God's blessing. In the six days that await God's work in Genesis 1, the land will become a paradise where the man and woman can enjoy God's blessing and live forever.

The description of the land in Genesis 1:2 fits well with the prophetic vision of the future. After God created the universe, the land lay empty, dark, and barren. It awaited God's call to light and life. Just as the light of the sun broke in upon the primeval darkness, heralding the dawn of God's first blessing (1:3), so also the prophets and the apostles mark the beginning of the new kingdom age of salvation with the light that breaks through the darkness (Isaiah 8:22–9:2; Matthew 4:13–17; John 1:5, 8–9). In that age, God's people will again enjoy the blessings of living in the promised land (Deuteronomy 30:1–5).

Later biblical texts make it clear that such a vision was already at work in the composition of the first chapter of Genesis. The future messianic salvation would be marked by a flowering of the "desert" wilderness (Isaiah 35:1–2). In the same way, in Genesis 1 God turned the "wilderness" into the garden of Eden.

God's final acts of salvation are thus foreshadowed in His initial acts of creation. The wilderness awaits its restoration. Henceforth the call to prepare for the coming day of salvation while waiting in the wilderness would become the hallmark of the prophets' vision of the future (Isaiah 40:3; Mark 1:4ff; Revelation 12:6, 14f).

There is darkness over the face of the waters in Genesis 1:2 because it is nighttime when God first begins to speak. This was not the first night and day in God's universe. Just as there were many rainbows before God put one in the clouds after the flood, so there were many nights before this one which began the week of events.

THE SPIRIT OF GOD

Modern biblical interpreters frequently translate the second half of verse 2 as "a mighty wind swept across the surface of the water" instead of "the Spirit of God" doing so. While it is true that the Hebrew word for "Spirit" can also mean "wind," there is little reason to depart from the traditional rendering of this part of the verse.

Most creationists believe in a "young earth" — that is, a world that is only about ten thousand years old. They believe a literal reading of Genesis 1 demands a "young earth." Progressive creationists and theistic evolutionists, conversely, hold that the universe is much older, as much as several billion years. They argue that we should not read Genesis 1 "literally," or at least in a "woodenly literal" fashion. They say we should let science determine the age of the universe and then interpret the Genesis narratives in light of their findings.

As Christians have debated the chronology of creation, the question of the age of the universe has become the center of a vigorous discussion among scientists, particularly astrophysicists working on the Hubble space telescope. While not long ago it was generally argued that the age of the universe was about fifteen billion years, it is now thought to be only half that old, about eight billion years. The adjustment resulted from new measurements taken by the Hubble space telescope. Scientists were able to determine that the speed with which the universe is now drifting apart is considerably greater than previously assumed. A higher speed for the expansion of the universe means less time was needed for it to have expanded to its present shape. Such estimates, of course, have wide margins of error. It is unlikely, however, that scientists will ever project that the earth is only ten thousand years old.

When creationists interpret the early chapters of Genesis to mean that the universe is quite "young," they realize that they will not likely find agreement from modern science. They are prepared and willing to reject the conclusions of modern science and seek to establish their own, alternative views of the age of the universe.

When progressive creationists, on the other hand, merge scientific theory with the Genesis account of creation, they run the risk of distorting the biblical message. Finding geological ages in the "days" of creation stretches the imagination of even many sympathetic readers. To suggest that the biblical writer intended the "days" in Genesis 1 to correspond to thousands, or millions, of years is a conspicuous attempt to harmonize the Bible and science. Though it may satisfy the demands of science, it can hardly claim to deal fairly with the text of Genesis.

The idea of God's Spirit as the active agency of His power is common in the Pentateuch and the rest of Scripture. When Israel was called upon to make God's tabernacle (Exodus 31), for example, they were to do so by means of God's Spirit (Exodus 31:3). It is therefore fitting that God would also do His "work" of creation by means of the Spirit.

THE SUNRISE

In verse 3, God said, "Let there be light." This verse raises serious questions about the coherence of the creation account in Genesis 1. There is "light" on the first day. That much is clear. The problem arises with the events of the fourth day; the text doesn't speak specifically of God making the sun until that day. Consequently, verse 3 is often understood to say that God created "light" before He created its source, the sun. And there is another, even more serious, point to be made here.

We have seen that the sun, moon, and stars were included in the phrase "heavens and earth" in Genesis 1:1. All the celestial bodies — including the sun, moon, and stars — were created "in the beginning." If this is so, why would God independently create "sunlight" in Genesis 1:2 after He had created the sun in 1:1? And how could God have created the sun both "in the beginning" and on the fourth day? As serious as these problems appear, I believe they disappear if we read the text as it was intended by its author.

The whole of the universe, including the sun, moon, and stars, were created "in the beginning." The "one day" of Genesis 1:3–5 was not the first day of God's creating the universe; rather, it was the first day of the week during which God prepared the promised land for the man and woman. Consequently, verse 3 does not describe the creation of light (or sunlight without the sun). In fact, it doesn't describe the "creation" of any kind of light. Rather, it describes the sunlight breaking through the darkness on the morning of the first day of the week. It is merely a description of the sunrise on the first day of the week.

When Genesis 1:3 says, "God said, 'Let there be light,'" it means, in effect, "God said, 'Let the sun rise.'" The phrase "let there be light" doesn't have to mean "let the light come into existence." Elsewhere in the Bible, this same phrase is used to describe the sunrise (see Exodus 10:23; Nehemiah 8:3; Genesis 44:3). It is especially fitting that God would initiate the "creation week" by calling forth the sunrise.

The text does not imply this was the first "sunrise." Since the sun had already been created in Genesis 1:1, the narrative assumes there may have been countless sunrises before this particular one. While all of them clearly were brought about by the Creator, in this case the writer makes the point explicit. In effect, the writer says to the reader, "God began this week of creation — as He does every week — by calling forth the sunlight to reveal His work." Here, then, on the first morning of the week in which God prepared the promised land, we see God beginning His work by bringing forth the sunrise. When the text says "and there was light," it means simply that the first day of that week had begun.

At the conclusion of this first day of the week the writer says, "and it was evening and it was morning." This shows that the beginning of the day was reckoned from the time of the evening darkness. "And it was morning" describes the sunrise marked by the phrase "and there was light" in verse 3.

A PROPER PLACE FOR HUMANS TO DWELL

On the first day of the week, God is shown preparing the land as a proper place for the man and woman to dwell. To imagine that God created the light on this day would be a misunderstanding. The narrative has clearly stated that God already created the sun "in the beginning." On this day, God called forth the sun to cast its bright light upon the land He was about "to make" for man. It is therefore altogether fitting that God's work began with a sunrise.

CHAPTER ELEVEN

THE SECOND DAY

GENESIS 1:6-8

Our understanding of the second day of creation is largely determined by how we view the author's perspective. The central question lies in how the author understood and used the Hebrew word "expanse" (*raqia*). Should we view this term along cosmological lines as a description of a major component of the universe (empty space), or do we view it within the more limited context of the promised land (the sky overhead)? What is the scope of the term? Biblical scholars have viewed this passage from both perspectives.

Franz Delitzsch understood the term *raqia* in largely cosmic dimensions. According to Delitzsch, the "expanse" was "the higher ethereal region, the so-called atmosphere...."[1] Though for Delitzsch the expanse was primarily that region of "sky" encircling the earth, for many others it included the whole realm of empty space throughout the entire universe. Today we would call it "outer space." In either case, the "expanse" is cast in cosmic and global dimensions.

The term "expanse" can also be understood in a more limited sense. If viewed simply within the context of the land promised to Abraham and the patriarchs, *raqia* can describe something immediate in the everyday experience of the author. For many biblical scholars, that has meant the immediate sky above our heads, or the surface upon which the clouds rest. John Calvin identified the expanse as just that.[2] He said the "waters above the expanse" were "the clouds suspended in the air."[3] If one wished to understand something about astronomy and the nature of the universe,

Calvin argued, he must go elsewhere than this passage. The passage teaches us only about what we see immediately around us.[4] It describes something in our world, not something in outer space.

We must be careful not to let our view of the structure of the universe nor the view of ancient cosmologists[5] control our understanding of the "expanse." We must seek clues from the biblical text itself.

IN SEARCH OF CLUES

One such clue is the purpose which the author himself assigns to the "expanse" in verse 6. He says the purpose of the expanse was "to separate water from water." The expanse was to separate the water above the land from the water below it.

A second textual clue is the name which the author later gives to the expanse. In verse 8 the expanse is named "the sky," or "the heavens."

Finally, we should look at how the term is used throughout the rest of the first chapter. The term is used to refer to the place where God put the sun, moon, and stars (1:14). It also refers to the place where the birds fly; in Genesis 1:20 we are told that the birds are to fly "upon the surface of the expanse of the sky."

In view of these distinct uses, is there a single word in English that would accommodate the Hebrew term "expanse"?

Ancient cosmological concepts such as a global "ceiling" or heavenly "vault" — which are often used to explain this term — clearly do not suit its use in Genesis 1:20. It is unlikely that the narrative has in view a "solid partition or vault that separates the earth from the waters above."[6] The birds do not fly upon the "heavenly vault." Such explanations, despite being drawn from ancient Near Eastern cosmologies, appear far too narrow for the present context in Genesis.

It appears more likely that Calvin was correct in his understanding of this text. The Genesis narrative pictures something within our everyday experience of the natural world. This is not an account for the astronomer or the astronaut; it is an account by someone who wishes to picture the world of our everyday lives, one whose feet are planted firmly on the ground. As a general term, the Hebrew word "expanse" thus denotes the place where the birds fly and where God has placed the lights of heaven. It is most similar in meaning to the English word "sky."

If we look for something within our everyday experience to correspond to the "waters above" the sky, it is likely we should see here a reference to the clouds overhead (as Calvin maintained). From the perspective of a person on land, that is where the water is held and from where it falls as rain. So on the second day of this week, God put clouds in the sky to provide rain for those dwelling in the land.

Modern "scientific creationists" usually identify the "expanse" with a primeval "water (or ice) canopy" which they believe once encased the earth in its outermost atmosphere. Henry Morris says, "The waters above [the firmament] must have been in the form of a vast blanket of invisible water vapor, translucent to the light from the stars but productive of a marvelous greenhouse effect [upon the earth]."[7] Such a canopy of water or vapor, they suggest, was the primary source of Noah's flood. Once precipitated by cosmic or volcanic disturbances, the "waters above the firmament" fell to earth and inundated the planet in the flood which we read about in Genesis 6–9. Thus, a major component of God's original creation is missing from the world today.

Such a reading of Genesis goes far beyond the dictates of the text. Though "scientific creationists" may be right about an original "water canopy" covering our planet, that is hardly the sense of "the expanse" in Genesis 1. That is not the sense in which it was read by later biblical authors. According to Psalm 148:4, for example, the "waters above the heavens" are not only still there in the psalmist's day, but God "set them in place forever and ever" (Psalm 148:6).

Biblically, the "waters above the heavens" are simply the clouds which provide rain for those dwelling in the land. Such a view is found many places in Scripture. The account of the flood in Genesis 7, for example, refers to the "windows of the sky." When those windows open, they pour forth the rain (7:11–12; cf. 2 Kings 7:2; Psalm 104:3; 147:8; 148:4). The rain comes from the "waters above" the land. It is held in the expanse by the clouds.

The writer of Proverbs 8:28 clearly understood the term *raqia* in Genesis 1 as a reference to the "clouds." In an obvious allusion to Genesis 1, he speaks of God's creative act of "establishing the clouds above and fixing securely the fountains of the deep." That was precisely what God did on the land on the second and third days. The same viewpoint is expressed in Psalm 104. Among the many poetic allusions to the Genesis account in Psalm 104, the psalmist speaks of God laying "the beams of his upper chambers on their waters" and making "the clouds his chariot" (104:3). The psalmist's use of poetic imagery does not mask the fact that he sees Genesis 1:6–7 as a description of God's making clouds over the land on the second day.

WHAT'S GOOD ABOUT IT?

It has often been noted that at the close of the second day, there is no mention of God's seeing that what He had made was "good." Yet after each of the other days, we are told explicitly that "God saw [what He had made, that] it was good." Why the omission on the second day? The reason is grounded in the primary meaning of the expression "good" in this chapter.

Throughout Genesis 1, the phrase "and God saw that it was good" is the author's way of saying that what God made was beneficial for mankind. The whole creation account is oriented toward God's creation of the man and the woman on the sixth day. That which is "good" in Genesis 1 is that which will benefit the man and woman.

Many commentators have observed that although God does not see anything "good" (for mankind) on the second day, on the third day we are told twice that God saw what He had created "was good." Why is this expression omitted on the second day but recorded twice on the third day? Because on the third day two distinct "works" of God are recounted: the appearance of the dry land and the fruit trees. Both of these were beneficial for mankind, and hence God saw that they were "good."

On the second day, however, nothing was made which directly benefited mankind. The land was still covered with water, and the clouds were formed, but mankind was not going to dwell in the water or fly through the clouds. Thus, there was no narrative reason for God to say that what He had made was "good." The term "good" in this chapter is not a statement about the inherent worth of God's work but about the divine purpose of His work. In this chapter something is considered "good" only if it directly benefits mankind.

A SUBTLE TENSION

One further observation should be made about the events of the second day. Many biblical scholars point to a subtle but significant tension between the statements of verses 6 and 7. Whereas verse 6 recounts the creation of the "expanse" by God's "word" alone ("And God said..."), verse 7

WHAT ABOUT THE WATER CANOPY?

On one point, creationists read what they feel is a particularly important part of their system into the creation account. The "firmament" or "expanse" in Genesis 1:6 — which later biblical writers apparently interpret as clouds — creationists interpret as a massive water (or ice) canopy which surrounded our entire planet before the flood. That canopy becomes a key element in their interpretation of Noah's catastrophic flood. It was the precipitation of that massive body of water which initiated Noah's flood and forever changed the face of our planet.

Since creationists attempt to prove their theory of a water canopy through accepted scientific means, their finding a biblical witness for it in Genesis 1 would appear to be nonessential to their system. It is, however, one of the few instances where their view of the flood can be linked to the biblical account of creation. It has thus become an important way in which creationists have attempted to gain some biblical warrant for their views.

---

looks at the same event as an actual activity of God ("So God made...").[8] First God spoke and then He acted. Throughout chapter 1 there is a similar alternation between the accounts of God's speaking and taking action.

Such an alternation of viewpoint has prompted many to suppose there is a serious duplication within the creation account (compare 1:11 with 1:12; 1:14 with 1:16; 1:24 with 1:25). That impression is heightened by the recurring expression "and it was so," which suggests that what God had commanded by His "word" had been accomplished. He spoke and it came to pass.[9]

A close reading of chapter 1 could make it appear that the author first recounted God's creative work as the *result* of His speaking ("And God said...and it was so") yet then recounted God's work as a *subsequent* act carried out to completion ("And God made...").

If such observations are valid, then the creation account appears to lack internal consistency and coherence. Is this correct? Or is there another, more appropriate, explanation for the apparent duplication which runs throughout the chapter?

THE NATURE OF NARRATIVE

One possible explanation lies in the nature of narrative texts. In recent years much thought and research has gone into this question. What makes narrative texts work? How are they structured? What kinds of strategies are at work within them? In narratives such as Genesis 1, a two-fold task always lies before the author.

First, it is his responsibility to recount the course of past events. In doing so he must maintain a consistent and continuous flow of events. Anyone who has ever written or told a story knows how difficult it can be to keep a steady story line. A good story is not easy to tell. Yet the biblical author's primary task is to keep the narrative going. How does he do that?

This is where the author's second task comes in. The author must supply the reader with more than the bare facts. In addition to the story, he must give explanatory comments on the events. He must express his opinion about and understanding of what is happening. He must "monitor" the reader's understanding of the events and attempt to "manage" the reader's appreciation of those events. He cannot leave the reader completely alone with the mere recounting of the events; he cannot allow the reader to form his own opinion of what is happening. He must guide the reader into a full appreciation and understanding.

If we turn to the narratives in Genesis, we see this was precisely what the author did in 2:24. After recounting the creation of the woman, the author momentarily sets aside the flow of narrative and addresses the reader directly with a word of advice and application. He says, "For this reason a man shall leave his father and mother and be united to his wife, and they will become one flesh." The author is helping the reader understand and apply the meaning of the events. He is directly "managing" the reader's understanding and response to the narrative.

In the past, little explicit attention was paid to such features of the biblical narrative. Yet the fact that most readers were unaware of such features didn't mean they were unaffected by them. On the contrary, the less one is aware of how the author is directing the understanding of a text, the more effective that process will be.

It has become increasingly apparent that the biblical narratives have such features to one degree or another.[10] And it is possible to explain some of the difficulties and irregularities of the Genesis creation story by looking for such "reader conscious" techniques within the narrative.

For example, Genesis 1:24 is a narrative account of God's work on the fifth day. The author first tells us that God spoke and the animals came into being ("And God said...and it was so"). That narrative is followed by a "reader oriented" comment. The narrator says, "God made the animals according to their own kind, and He saw that it was good" (1:25). Presumably the purpose of such a comment was to assure the reader that God made the animals — no one else. The comment also emphasizes that God made the animals according to "their own kind," a key theme in this chapter which finds its ultimate focal point in the one major exception:

the creation of man according to the image of God. The man and woman were not made "after their own kind" but were created "in the image of God."

When we read Genesis 1 with these "reader oriented" comments in mind, several problems are quickly solved. Such comments not only account for the duplications within this chapter, but more importantly they allow for a clearer understanding of the author's overall intention.

On the second day, for example, the text says that God's call for an "expanse" was answered only when God himself "made" the expanse. The "expanse," in other words, was not *created* from nothing on the second day; it was *made* by God on that day, specifically for the waters over the land. Earlier we saw that the Hebrew term "made" means "to set aright" or "make suitable." That is what the writer wants to bring out in the apparent repetitions in verses 6 and 7.

When we note these features of the text, we suddenly see that these narratives have "depth." They tell of past events and speak directly to contemporary readers about those events. By monitoring the reading of his own text, the author reveals his chief interest in the events. At each point he can be seen preparing the reader to properly understand the narrative. When such an understanding of the nature of the biblical narrative is applied to Genesis 1:14–17 (which records the events of the fourth day), many major difficulties are removed. See page 134 for further discussion of this feature of the fourth day.

IN SUMMARY: HOW'S THAT AGAIN?

On the second day God prepared the sky with clouds to provide rain for the land. The rain would prepare the land for producing vegetation on the next day. The sky was still empty of life on the second day but would be filled with all kinds of "flying creatures" on the fifth day (Genesis 1:20).

There is no reason to suppose that the events of the second day have any wider point of view than the rest of the chapter itself. That is, the events of the second day tell us what God did in preparing the promised land. We know from the first verse that the sky and land already existed at this time. Moreover, we know from the merism in Genesis 1:1 ("heavens and earth") that the earth had already been populated with "flying creatures" in "the beginning." So in this text we are viewing only that which God did to prepare the promised land for mankind.

CHAPTER TWELVE

THE THIRD DAY

O n the third day we see God carrying out two distinct acts: He prepares "the land and the seas," and He furnishes the land with fruit trees.

Unlike the work of the second day, both acts are called "good." They are "good" because both were accomplished for mankind's benefit. Both acts relate to the preparation of the promised land.

PREPARATION OF THE LAND

The narrative of the separation of the waters and the preparation of the land is to be read in light of the subsequent accounts of the flood (Genesis 6–9) and the parting of the Red Sea (Exodus 14–15). In all three accounts, the waters are cast as an obstacle to man's inhabiting and enjoying "the good land." In each case, the water must be removed before God's people can enjoy His gift of the land. But as we learn in the account of the flood and of the Red Sea, the waters were also God's instrument of judgment upon those who did not walk in His way.

The author of Genesis 1 was thus not merely recounting past events, he was also building a case for the importance of obeying God's will. In his account of creation, the author begins with a simple picture of God's mighty power at work, harnessing the great sea on behalf of man's "good." The later flood account is a bitter reminder of the other side of God's power as the waters become an instrument of judgment.

To appropriately understand this narrative from the author's point of view, we should not think of the "oceans" when we read that God named the "pools of water" the "seas" in Genesis 1:10. In Hebrew, any "pool" of water — regardless of the size — is called a "sea."[1]

The passage itself makes it clear that we shouldn't have oceans in mind when it describes the waters being gathered together "into one place." The waters didn't gather into "many places," but only "one place." The text is very precise here. It clearly views the "pools of water" as those "seas" which cover the promised land even today, namely the "sea" of Galilee, the dead "sea," and the great "sea" to the west, the Mediterranean Sea. In Hebrew, each of these "pools of water" is called a "sea." In the biblical writer's understanding of the waters which fill those "seas," they were all gathered together in "one place" — that is, in (and alongside of) the promised land.

At this point in the narrative, all these waters are not yet teeming with life. They must be filled with appropriate creatures — the fish and "swarming creatures" of the fifth day.

FRUIT TREES APPEAR

It is often overlooked that no forms of vegetation are mentioned in Genesis 1:9–11 other than fruit trees. While most English translations give the impression that God created "all kinds of trees" on the third day, the Hebrew text is clear that God made only the fruit trees on that day. We learn from the conclusion of the story that the fruit trees were created for mankind.

Genesis 1:30 informs us that other forms of vegetation were given to the animals, but it doesn't say when those plants were created. In fact, Genesis 1 doesn't record God specifically creating the plants which He later gave to the animals to eat. As far as the third day is concerned, we are told only that the fruit trees were made on that day. So when were those plants ("every green plant") made?

In the logic of the whole of Genesis 1, we are to assume that those plants were already created for the animals during "the beginning" of verse 1. This is yet another clue that the remainder of Genesis 1 doesn't describe the creation of the universe and the world, but rather concerns itself with the preparation of the promised land. God didn't have to create "all kinds of trees" and vegetation on the third day because they were already created "in the beginning." Only fruit trees had to be created in the land (Genesis 1:29) in order to provide food for the man and woman who were to be created on the sixth day.

Therefore in His second act on the third day, God furnishes the land with fruit trees. It is likely that the author intended a connection to be drawn between God's furnishing the land with fruit trees in chapter 1 and His furnishing the garden with trees "good for food" in chapter 2. This is yet another clue that the two accounts in Genesis 1 and 2 are indeed about the same work of creation and that the "land" of chapter 1 should be understood as the "garden" of chapter 2.

CHAPTER THIRTEEN

THE FOURTH DAY

T he narration of events on the fourth day raises several questions, making this perhaps the most difficult section of the account of creation. It has been widely held that on this day God created the sun, moon, and stars. A simple reading of the text in virtually any English translation would almost certainly lead to that conclusion.

But does the text actually say that the sun, moon, and stars were created on the fourth day? I don't believe it does. Yet if the text *did* say those heavenly bodies were created on the fourth day, a major problem would confront us. How could the universe — which includes the sun, moon, and stars — have been created "in the beginning" (1:1) and also on the fourth day? And how could the author speak of a "day and night" during the first three days of creation if the sun had not yet been created? Furthermore, are we to understand that plants and vegetation were created on the third day, before the creation of the sun?

EARLY EXPLANATIONS

Interpreters of Genesis 1 have long faced these problems, and many scholars have attempted to resolve the difficulties. One of the greatest biblical scholars of the last century, C. F. Keil, took a common approach to the problem. According to Keil, the "heavens and earth" were created "in the beginning" (1:1) yet were not "completed" until the fourth day.[1]

Keil's explanation was foreshadowed in Calvin's comments on this text. According to Calvin, "the world was not perfected at its very commencement, in the manner in which it is now seen, but that it was created an empty chaos of heaven and earth."[2] As Calvin understood it, this "empty chaos" was simply that, an empty space. It was filled on the fourth day with the sun, moon, and stars. Calvin's view was similar to that of the medieval Jewish scholar Rashi: "[The sun, moon, and stars] were created," says Rashi, "on the first day, but on the fourth day [God] commanded that they be placed in the sky."[3]

Another common attempt to resolve the inherent difficulties of the fourth day is the "Restitution Theory" or "Gap Theory," which is presented in the Scofield Bible (as well as much earlier works). According to the Scofield Bible, "The sun and moon were created 'in the beginning.' The 'light' of course came from the sun, but the vapor diffused the light. Later the sun appeared in an unclouded sky."[4] According to the Scofield view, the sun, moon, and stars were all created in 1:1, but they could not be seen from the earth until the fourth day.

This view has recently been revived and modified by Hugh Ross. According to Ross, "for some time after the transformation of the Earth's atmosphere to an oxidizing one, air temperature and pressure variations and a very humid condition would have prevented any break in the cloud cover. Volcanic activity also may have contributed to this cloudy condition.... Through time, changes in these various environmental features — stabilization of air temperature and pressure, consumption of carbon dioxide by plants, and decrease in volcanic activity — probably all contributed to breaking the cloud cover. The result? The appearance of 'light in the expanse of the sky to separate the day from the night...to serve as signs to mark seasons and days and years' (verse 14)."[5]

Each of these interpretations seeks to avoid what appears to be the plain meaning of the text — that the sun, moon, and stars were created on the fourth day. Each view adjusts the sense of the Hebrew verb "to make" in Genesis 1:16 so that it harmonizes with the statement of the first verse, that God created the universe in the beginning.

Some biblical scholars have dealt with this problem by making

Genesis 1:1 into a title for the entire chapter. We discussed (and rejected) this approach earlier in the book.[6] Yet if Genesis 1:1 were a title for the whole chapter, there would be no inherent difficulty with the idea of God's making the sun, moon, and stars on the fourth day. Verse 1 would then merely anticipate that aspect of God's creation. The whole chapter would describe God's creating all the universe, and on the fourth day He made the sun, moon, and stars. There would thus be no internal inconsistency in understanding the fourth day as the time when the heavenly bodies were created.

A BETTER WAY?

I am convinced there is a better way to look at this text, a way which provides a satisfactory and coherent reading of both Genesis 1:1 and 1:14ff. First, we must be clear that the merism "heavens and earth" in Genesis 1:1 means "universe" or "cosmos"[7] (see chapter 4). That includes the sun, moon, and stars. So the starting point of our understanding of 1:14ff is that the whole universe, including the sun, moon, and stars, was created "in the beginning" (1:1). That means they couldn't have been created on the fourth day.

Second, we should consider the Hebrew grammar and syntax of verse 14. When verse 14 is compared to verse 6, it's clear that the two verses don't have the same meaning. The way verse 6 is written in Hebrew suggests that when God said, "Let there be an expanse," He was "making" an expanse over the land, an expanse which had not been there before. As I argued previously, the Hebrew word "to make" (Genesis 1:7) means "to set aright," "to fix," or "to set in order." Thus on the second day, the sky over the land had to be "set aright" so as to be beneficial for humanity. Before God said, "Let there be an expanse" (1:6), the sky over the land was not fit for human beings in the land. Specifically that meant on the second day that there were no clouds to hold water to nourish the land for mankind.

Although the Hebrew verbal construction in verse 14 is significantly different from verse 6, our English translations don't always reflect that difference. In the Hebrew text of verse 14, God does *not* say, "Let there be lights in the expanse to separate the day and night…" as if there were no lights before His command and afterward they came into being. Rather, according to the Hebrew text, God said, "Let the lights in the expanse be for separating the day and night…." God's command, in other words, *assumes that the lights already exist* in the expanse. To be sure, there has been no mention of these "lights" earlier in Genesis 1, but their existence is assumed in the expression "heavens and earth" in Genesis 1:1.[8]

The meaning of God's command in verse 14 is that the "lights" which were created "in the beginning" now are to serve "to separate the day and night" and "to be signs to mark the seasons and days of the year." Given the difference between the Hebrew syntax of verse 6[9] and verse 14[10], the narrative suggests that the author did not understand his account of the fourth day to be an account of the creation of the lights but merely a statement of their purpose. The narrative assumes that the heavenly lights already were created "in the beginning."

BUT WHAT DID GOD DO?

In reading Genesis 1, many of us are accustomed to thinking that on each day of the week God "made" something in particular. Thus, we often speak of the various "acts" of creation on each day. We look for what God "did" on each day, and we assume this means He "made" something.

Such a view, however, does not conform to the statements of the account itself. While it is true that on most of the days God does "make" something (at least in the broad sense of the term), a more fundamental observation of the events of each day suggests that He did something much more significant.

What the writer wants most to show in this narrative is not that on each day God "made" something, but that on each day God "said" something. The predominant view of God in this chapter is that He is a God who speaks. His word is powerful. As the psalmist who had read this chapter said, "By the word of the Lord the heavens were made" (Psalm

33:6). Thus, often when God speaks, He creates. But that is not always the case in this chapter.

On the subject of creation, there can be no real conflict between science, history, and the Bible. The conflict exists at the level of the assumptions which science, history, and the Bible make about "pre-scientific" matters. And all of them make pre-scientific assumptions about the ultimate nature of the world.

At the level of those assumptions, however, the Bible will often be in serious conflict with the assumptions of science and history. And it is at that level we can discuss the possibility of resolution between the Bible and science.

Yet the resolution of that conflict should come not from showing the Bible to be more scientific than science or more historical than history. (Both approaches, incidentally, have been widely used by evangelical biblical scholars and scientists.) Rather, it should come by showing that the assumptions laid down by the Bible are more valid than those laid down by either modern science or modern historiography.

Three major belief systems reflect widely varying assumptions about the nature of the world:

Theism is the belief in a creator God who is transcendent over and governor of the material universe. Only God is eternal. The material world, which He created and governs, had a beginning and, if He so wills, has an end. God is active not only in creation but continues to be involved in the world. A theistic view of scientific matters would allow for miracles, and a theistic view of history would allow for providence, God's active control of the events of history.

Materialism is the belief that all reality exists in the form of matter and energy. The world can and should be explained solely on the basis of the interaction of matter and energy.

Naturalism is the belief that the only forces at work in the world are those inherent in the physical world, including the active role of human will. History must be explained solely in those terms. There is no place for the activity of a transcendent God.

Obviously, whichever system is chosen largely determines one's conclusions about "truth." The historical position of Christianity and the Bible has been, of course, Theism.

For example, on the fourth day God speaks, but He does not "make" anything. On this day God "makes a proclamation" about that which He has already created (the sun, moon, and stars). Certainly it is true that the sun, moon, and stars were already marking the day and night. Potentially, at least, they were fit to mark the seasons, days, and years. But just as the significance of the rainbow was given long after it had been created (Genesis 9:13), so also God announced His purpose for creating the sun, moon, and stars, on the fourth day — long after they had been created.

So if one asks, "Did God *do* anything on the fourth day?" the answer from the text itself is yes. Just as He did on every other day, God "spoke" on the fourth day. The writer is intent on showing that the whole world depends on the word of God. The world owes not merely its existence to the word of God, but also its order and purpose. It is thus no small matter when the biblical writer shows us that on the fourth day God proclaimed His plan and purpose for creating the celestial bodies. He created them to serve humanity in the day when they began to dwell in God's land.

The structure of verses 15 and 16 also suggests the writer's emphasis on the word of God. At the end of verse 15, the author places one of his concluding statements — "and it was so." As was true in verses 6 and 7, this expression marks the end of the author's narrative of past events and the beginning of his "comment" on those events. Thus, verse 16 is not an account of God's actions on the fourth day. Rather, it is a comment on what God said on that day. The remark is directed to the reader, drawing out the significance of what was previously reported.

The author's comment in Genesis 1:16 explains, first, that God alone created the sun, moon, and stars. This verse looks back to God's creating "the universe" in Genesis 1:1. Verse 16 could be translated, "So God (and not anyone else) made the lights and put them in the sky." This does not say *when* God created "the lights," but given the overall meaning of Genesis 1:1, it is naturally assumed that they were created "in the beginning." Behind this narrative there is a deep concern to emphasize that God alone created the lights of the heavens and no one else is to be given the glory and honor due to Him. The author's comment in Genesis 1:16 also states *why* God created the lights in the heavens. The purpose was to divide day and night and to mark the "seasons, days, and years." Both of these concerns form the central focus of chapter 1: God alone is the Creator of all things and worthy of the worship of His people.

The fact that God announced the purpose for the lights on the fourth day does not mean they had not already been performing that purpose since "the beginning." The point of the narrative is to show that God waited until the fourth day to explain His purpose for creating the sun, moon, and stars in "the beginning."

Why did God wait until the fourth day to announce the purpose of the sun, moon, and stars? The answer lies in the overall structure of the creation account. The parallel relationship between the events of the first three days and the last three days has long been recognized. On the first three days, God's activity focused consecutively on the sky, the seas, and the land. On the last three days, God's activities again focused on those three realms. On the fourth day, God commanded the sun, moon, and stars to distinguish day and night and all the signs and seasons (1:14–15). On the fifth day, God commanded the seas to swarm with fish and sea creatures, and on the sixth day, He commanded the land to bring forth animal life.

Having prepared, in consecutive order, the skies, the seas, and the land on the first three days, God, on the last three days, proclaimed the purpose for those things which were to fill the skies, the seas, and the land. God waited, therefore, until the fourth day to make known His plan for the signs that were to fill the skies.

TO SUM UP

God did not make the sun, moon, and stars on the fourth day. He created them "in the beginning." On the fourth day God proclaimed His purpose in making those celestial bodies. They were to serve mankind in the land as signs of God's power and as reminders of the seasons, days, and years, when His creatures were to worship him.

CHAPTER FOURTEEN

THE FIFTH DAY

GENESIS 1:20–23

On the fifth day God populated the land with many kinds of living creatures. The text divides the fifth day into two stages extending into the sixth day.

On the fifth day God created the creatures of the sea and the birds (or more precisely, the flying creatures). On the sixth day (1:24–28) God created the land creatures, which included men and women.

A FAMILIAR PATTERN

The narrative of the fifth day follows a familiar pattern. In verse 20, God speaks ("And God said…"), and in verse 21, God acts ("So God created…"). As in the other sections of this narrative, careful attention to detail can help us see clearly the author's overall purpose.

First, the word translated "created" in this passage is the same Hebrew word used in the first verse: *bara*. It is used six times in the creation account (1:1, 21, 27; 2:3). Elsewhere in Genesis 1 the word *asah* ("to make") is used to describe God's actions. Why is the verb *bara* used to describe God's actions on the fifth day? In particular, why are the "great sea creatures" (1:21) singled out by the use of this special term?

One suggestion is that the use of the word "to create" is intended to mark the beginning of a new stage in the creation account. For the first time we hear of the creation of the "living beings," a group distinct from the vegetation and physical world of the previous days. Each new stage in creation is thus marked by the special Hebrew verb *bara*, "to create:" the universe (1:1); the living creatures (1:20–21); and humanity (1:26–27).

The use of *bara* on the fifth day also may be related to the notion of the "blessing" (*berakah*), which is mentioned for the first time on that day. The word *berakah* is clearly intended as a wordplay in Hebrew on the verb *bara*. It is significant that the word "to create" also occurs on the sixth and seventh days, where again it is linked by means of a wordplay to the Hebrew word "blessing."[1]

There may be yet another reason for the use of the word "to create" on the fifth day. It may serve to answer an important question raised by Genesis 1:1. If Genesis 1:1 states that God created the universe "in the beginning," and if that means God created the plants and animals at the same time, then why does God create more animals on the fifth and sixth days? This question is actually another version of the question regarding the apparent creation of the sun, moon, and stars on the fourth day. The answer is the same in both cases. Genesis 1:1 is clear that God created the sun, moon, and stars — as well as all the animals on earth — "in the beginning."

As we will suggest in the following discussion, Genesis 1:21 is best explained as a comment on verse 20. It is a comment to remind the reader that God "created" all kinds of animals "in the beginning" (1:1). Though, as we shall see, God did create "some" animals on the fifth day, He had already created "all" the various kinds of animals "in the beginning." The use of the word *bara* thus turns the readers' attention back to the comprehensive statement about creation in 1:1.

A NOTICEABLE DISTINCTION

It is important to observe that within the Hebrew text a distinction is made between what God does on the fifth day (1:20) and the author's comment in the next verse. A close look at the fifth day reveals the significance of these two quite different types of statements.

The first type is represented by instances in which God commands the water to be filled with swarming creatures (1:20a) and the sky to be filled with flying creatures (1:20b). God's commands here do not call these creatures into existence, as if they did not exist previously. Rather, they simply assign the creatures to their proper domains, the waters and the sky. The narrative assumes there are already swarming creatures and birds.

An important observation should be made about God's command to the birds. It is a small detail, but in this narrative hardly a detail is unimportant. God commands the birds to fly "over the land, upon the surface of the expanse of the sky." The important observation is that the birds are to fly "over the land." It appears obvious from this statement that God is not so much "creating" the birds as He is filling the skies over "the land" which He has just prepared for them. What land does the narrative have in mind? The promised land.

The same point should be made regarding God's filling the "waters" with fish and other sea creatures (1:20a). These "waters" are apparently to be understood as the "seas" which God formed in the land on the third day (1:10). In the viewpoint of the original author, the purpose of God's commands is not the *creation* of various animals over all the earth, but the specific task of populating the land He is preparing for mankind. Here we see God filling the promised land with various kinds of animals that were already created in "the beginning."

If this is a correct understanding of Genesis 1:20, then the verb "to create" is used in verse 21 as a comment to the reader. It reminds the reader of an important part of the overall narrative — God "created" all the animals. The author does not say God created all the animals on the fifth day; he merely says it was God who created all the animals and that now He commands some to fill the waters and the skies over the promised land. When did God "create" those animals? The logic of the narrative and the use of the Hebrew word *bara* lead us back to the initial statement of Genesis 1: "In the beginning God created [*bara*] the universe." At that time God "created" the animals that now are brought into the newly prepared waters and skies of the promised land.[2]

There is a further question about the creatures mentioned on the fifth day. Why does the author mention specifically the "huge sea creatures" in Genesis 1:21? Does that kind of creature have a special significance? This question has never been successfully answered.

Some interpreters have seen in these "huge creatures" the remnants of an ancient myth about dragons and sea monsters. Medieval maps were characteristically decorated with "sea monsters" in the remotest regions of the oceans. Such mythological creatures were known to the biblical writers as is clear from Isaiah 27:1, which speaks of God's slaying "the monster of the sea" (NIV). We must be careful, however, not to read the poetic imagery of Isaiah back into the narratives of Genesis 1.

It is more likely that the Genesis narratives have a specific type of animal in mind and are not referring to a mythological creature. The Hebrew word used in Genesis 1:21 occurs also in Exodus 7:9–12. When Moses threw his staff down before the pharaoh, it became a "snake" (NIV) or, as some commentators suggest (correctly, I think), a "crocodile." The point is that the Pentateuch doesn't consider these animals as mythological creatures but simply as large aquatic animals — snakes or crocodiles. Granted this, why does the author feel it necessary to mention specifically these large animals?

If we see verse 21 as a comment directing the reader back to Genesis 1:1, then the mention of "huge sea creatures" plays an important role in the meaning of the whole chapter.

We should first note that it is not merely the "huge sea creatures" that are "created" in Genesis 1:21. The text also says that the "living creatures that swarm in the waters" and the birds, or flying creatures, were also "created." That makes three distinct groups of creatures which the writer reminds us were "created" (bara) "in the beginning."

By listing these three distinct groups of creatures, the writer of Genesis 1 provides an interpretive summary of one of the implications of the phrase "heavens and earth" in 1:1. The phrase "heavens and earth" means that "all the animals" (from the largest sea creatures to the tiniest swarming creatures and the birds) were created "in the beginning."

What then is the focus of God's work on the fifth day? It is simply to populate the promised land with the various creatures that were created "in the beginning." The picture of the events of this day are reminiscent of God's filling the waters and skies of Egypt with swarms of water creatures in Moses' day. When Moses extended his staff over the Nile River, as he was commanded by God to do, the text says, "the Nile was to swarm with frogs" (Exodus 8:3). These are the same Hebrew terms which are found in Genesis 1:20. When Moses followed God's command, the text again says, "the frogs came up [from the Nile] and covered the land" (Exodus 8:6).

Did God create frogs then and there in Egypt for the first time? Clearly not. The Egyptian magicians even duplicated this act with their secrets arts (Exodus 8:7). Did God create frogs instantaneously at that moment and for that occasion? Perhaps, but we must rest content with the fact that the narrative simply does not tell us. As far as the narrative is concerned, there could have been a natural explanation for the sudden appearance of the frogs. Whatever the case may have been, the narrative is clear on one point: The frogs were there at God's command.

The narrative in Genesis 1:20–21 is clear on the same point. God spoke, and frogs, fish, and birds came from somewhere and filled the skies and waters of the land. There is no need to suppose that these creatures did not already exist as a result of God's work of creation "in the beginning." On the fifth day God simply populated the "land" with those creatures. Verse 21 reinforces that interpretation by reminding us that God had, "in the beginning," created these creatures with which He was now populating the land.

CHAPTER FIFTEEN

THE SIXTH DAY

T he account of the creation of the land creatures on the sixth day distinguishes two types of creatures: the "living creatures" that dwell upon the land, and humankind. In turn, the "living creatures" of the land are divided into three groups: "livestock," "creatures that move along the ground," and "wild animals." Human beings are distinguished as "male" and "female."

AN IMPORTANT CLARIFICATION

Once again the author begins with a divine command ("And God said…") in verse 24, and then he follows with a comment to the reader ("So God made…") in verse 25. On first sight, the comment in verse 25 doesn't appear to add significantly to verse 24. However, a comparison of these verses with Genesis 1:11 and 12, which are similar, shows that verse 25 does add an important clarification. In 1:11, God had said, "Let the land produce vegetation." In the comment which followed (1:12), the author has added, "So the land produced the vegetation.…"

What was the point of that comment in verse 12? Apparently it was to say that the land, not God, produced the vegetation. In verses 24 and 25, however, there is a marked shift in emphasis. Verse 24 has reported a command similar to verse 11: "Let the land produce living creatures.…" But the comment which follows in verse 25 stresses a quite different feature — it was God who made the living creatures, not merely the land: "So God made the wild animals.…"

Apparently the author wanted to show that although the command was the same for creating the vegetation and the living creatures on land, there was an important distinction between the origin of the two forms of life. Vegetation was produced from the land, but the living creatures were made by God himself. "Life" stems from God and is to be distinguished from the rest of the physical world.

A SERIES OF SUBTLE CONTRASTS

The creation of human beings is set apart from the previous acts of creation by a series of subtle contrasts.

First, the creation of mankind is marked in verse 26 by the usual "And God said...." However, the words of God which follow are not the expected impersonal command: "Let there be a man...." Instead, the words are in first person; they are the personal expression of the will of God: "Let us make man...." The contrast is striking and shows the central importance the narrative attaches to the creation of the man and woman. The effect would be the same as if a speaker in the midst of a formal presentation suddenly broke the cadence of his words and began to talk personally to the audience.

Second, throughout the previous account each living creature has been made "according to its own kind." Yet it is specifically noted that the man and woman were made "according to the likeness of God." Man's likeness is not shared merely with all other human beings; rather, he shares a likeness with his own Creator!

On the day he was created, the biblical Adam did not rub his eyes and say "Where am I?" or "Who am I?" Such questions may be common today, but they were not asked by the first man at his creation. The biblical narratives represent him as someone at home in his world, someone who immediately understands all that he sees in the world around him. Yet this is not surprising if indeed he was created in the image of God.

Third, the creation of man is specifically described as the creation of "male and female." Up to this point in the creation account, the author has not considered gender an important feature to stress. For human beings, however, it is important. Thus the narrative stresses that God created "male and female."

Fourth, throughout Genesis 1 only humanity was given dominion over God's creation. This dominion is expressly stated as being over all other living creatures, whether of the sky, sea, or land. Why has the author singled out man in this way? An obvious answer is that he intended to portray man as special. He is a creature marked off from the rest of God's works. There appears to be more to it than that, however.

Man is not merely different from the rest of God's creatures; man is like God. Behind the portrayal of the creation of man lies the larger purpose of the author within the Pentateuch. Man is a creature; that much is clear from the narrative. But man is also a special creature. He is made in the image and likeness of God.

THE AGE OF HUMANKIND

Both the Bible and modern science place the origin of actual human life (homo sapiens sapiens) very late on the geological time clock. When reckoned by strict archaeological evidence, human beings begin to show up only about 30,000 years ago.[1] Compared to the millions of years that science says all other species of life have existed on earth, human beings arrived on the scene only yesterday.

When the genetic codes of human beings are examined, the time at which they appear to have arrived on the scene grows to 200,000–270,000 years ago. But both time periods are extremely recent, scientifically speaking, and remarkably surprising for an evolutionary theory of human origin. The study of the genetic codes of both our male and female ancestors has recently revealed that all human beings alive today can be traced back to a single male and female.[2]

Despite the great similarities in genetic structure between humans and the rest of the animal chain, there appear to be no immediate or even distant genetic ancestors to modern humans. The notion that human beings evolved from a lower form of "human" or sub-human life has therefore become extremely problematic. Today there are no inherently plausible evolutionary explanations for the origin of human beings. They merely arrive on the scene, very late in the process, with no discernible immediate antecedents.

There have been many attempts to explain the plural forms in Genesis 1:26: "Let *us* make man in our image, according to *our* likeness."[1] Westermann summarizes the explanations under four headings:

1. The plural refers to the Trinity.

2. The plural refers to God and His heavenly court of angels.

3. The plural is an attempt to avoid the idea of an immediate resemblance of humans to God.

4. The plural expresses the deliberation on God's part as He sets out to create man.[2]

The singulars in verse 27 (see also 5:1) rule out explanation 2, that the plurals refer to a heavenly court of angels. Note that in verse 27, humanity's creation is said to be "in God's image" with no mention of the image of the angels. In the same verse it says God created mankind "in His image." Surely such statements rule out any notion of angels. Nehemiah 9:6 may also be an attempt to ensure that the plurals of Genesis 1:26 aren't interpreted as referring to angels. In Nehemiah 9:6 we see that God "alone" made the heavens and earth, thus ruling out any angelic participation in mankind's creation.

Explanations 3 and 4 are both possible within the context. Neither explanation, however, is specifically supported by the context. Where we do find unequivocal deliberation within the biblical narratives (as in Genesis 18:17), the singular is used, not the plural: "Shall *I* hide from Abraham what *I* am about to do?" As Westermann has stated, explanation 1 is "a dogmatic judgment," though this fact alone does not automatically rule it out; it may be correct even though it is dogmatic. The author of Genesis 1 may, in fact, have intended such a dogmatic judgment. The important question is whether that judgment runs counter to the passage itself. In the last analysis, we must go back to the text to decide how we are to understand the plurals in verse 26.

If we seek an answer from the immediate context, we should turn to the next verse for our clues. In verse 27 it is stated twice that man was created in God's image and a third time that man was created "male and female." The same pattern is found in Genesis 5:1–2a: "When God created man…male and female he created them." The singular Hebrew word "man" is used to speak of the creation of a plurality, male and female.

In a similar way, the one God created man through an expression of His plurality: "Let us make man in our image." Following that clue, the divine plurality expressed in verse 26 can be seen as an anticipation of the human plurality of the man and woman. In that way, the human relationship between a man and woman becomes a witness to God's own personal relationship within the Godhead. It is for that reason we find in the next chapter that God put the man into the garden to worship and obey Him (Genesis 2:15, see earlier discussion). Karl Barth asks, "Could anything be more obvious than to conclude from this clear indication that the image and likeness of the being created by God signifies existence in confrontation, i.e., in this confrontation, in the juxtaposition and conjunction of man and man which is that of male and female, and then to go on to ask against this background in what the original and prototype of the divine existence of the Creator consists?"[3]

THE BLESSING

The importance of God's "blessing" the man and woman in verse 28 cannot be overlooked. Throughout the remainder of the book of Genesis and the Pentateuch, the "blessing" remains a central theme.[4] The living creatures already have been blessed on the fifth day (verse 22); thus the author's view of the blessing extends beyond humanity to all of God's living creatures. In verse 28 man is also included in God's blessing.

The blessing in these verses is primarily the gift of children ("posterity"). God said, "Be fruitful and multiply and fill the land" (1:28). Thus already the fulfillment of the blessing is tied to man's "seed" and the notion of "life" — two themes that will later dominate the narratives of Genesis.

CHAPTER SIXTEEN

THE SEVENTH DAY

GENESIS 2:1–4a

The author set the seventh day apart from the first six not only by stating specifically that God "sanctified" it, but also by markedly changing the style of his account. On this day God did not "speak" nor did He "work," as He had on the previous days. God "blessed" and "sanctified" the seventh day, but He did not "work" on that day. The reader is left with a somber and repeated reminder of a single fact: God did not work on the seventh day. While little else is recounted, it is repeated three times that God did not work.

The author surely intended by this to emphasize God's "rest." It is likely, as well, that the author intended the reader to understand the account of the seventh day in light of the "image of God" theme of the sixth day.

If the purpose of pointing to the "likeness" between man and his Creator was to call upon the reader to be more like God (see Leviticus 11:45), then it is significant that the seventh day stresses what the writer elsewhere so ardently calls upon the reader to do: "rest" on the seventh day (cf. Exodus 20:8–11).

This is another case in which the author points to the past as a picture of the future. At important points along the way, the author returns to the theme of God's "rest" as a reminder of the blessing that lies ahead (2:15;[1] 5:29; 8:4; 19:16;[2] Exodus 20:11; Deuteronomy 5:14; 12:10; 25:19). Later biblical writers continued to see a parallel between God's "rest" in creation and the future "rest" that awaits the faithful (Psalm 95:11; Hebrews 3:11).

The creation account closes its first segment with a beautiful picture of

God and His people enjoying a Sabbath rest in "His land." There is no hint of the tragic events that await them. In God's rest, the time which began in the first verse of this narrative seems to come to a complete halt. The second chapter of Genesis retells the events of this first week to further stress the fellowship which was possible between God and his newly created humanity. The garden is planted within the boundaries of the promised land. The gold and precious stones, much like the materials of the later tabernacle and temple, set it off as a place worthy of divine glory. With the land prepared, the universe was "complete" (Genesis 2:1) and God's work of creation was "finished" (Genesis 2:2).

THE END OF THE STORY

Such is the end of our story of the creation account in Genesis 1. When viewed from the perspective of the entire Pentateuch, the Genesis 1 account of creation is both literal and historical. It begins with a far-reaching statement of God's power and majesty. It was He who created the universe we see around us today.

The account, however, quickly turns the reader's attention to the central focus of the Pentateuch, God's gift of the land. During a period of a single human week, God "made" that land. With the exception of the human beings on the sixth day, God did not "create" the land or anything in the land during that week. He "ordered" the land, making it a place where the man and woman could dwell. On the night He began His work, the land was uninhabitable. As He began to speak, however, the land took on those characteristics which would make it a "good" place for God's human creatures.

We might well imagine that when God began His work of preparing the land, there were already many places on earth suitable for their habitation. The writer of the Pentateuch, however, is interested only in God's preparation of the promised land. That is where God had promised to bless His people, Israel and, through them, the rest of humanity. That is where God began His work, and that is where God would one day in the future complete it.

CHAPTER SEVENTEEN

THE CREATION OF HUMANITY, TAKE TWO

GENESIS 2

As we have already stressed, it is important to read chapter 2 as an integral part of chapter 1. It seems clear that the author intended the second chapter to be read closely with the first and the events in each chapter to be identified as part of the same event. Thus at the start of the second chapter, the author explicitly returns to the place and time of the first chapter, and there he links the two: "When the LORD God made the land and the sky...." (2:4b).

We would expect that the author's central theological interests in chapter 1 would be continued in chapter 2. In chapter 1 his central interest was the creation of humanity in God's "image." Therefore we may expect to find in the second chapter a continuation of the theme of "likeness" between man and the Creator.

THE CREATION OF MAN

Chapter 2 begins with a description of the condition of the land before the creation of mankind. In this respect it resembles the description of the land in 1:2. The text focuses on those parts of the land that were to be directly affected by the Fall (3:8–24). The narrative points out that before man was created (verse 7), the effects of his rebellion and the Fall had not yet made their mark on the land. In the subsequent narratives, each description of the land in verses 4b–6 is specifically linked with some result of the Fall. The "shrub of the field" and "plant of the field," for example, are not referring to the "vegetation" of chapter 1. Rather, they anticipate the "thorns and thistles" and "plants of the field" which were to come as a result of the curse (3:18).

In the same way, when the narrative states that the Lord God had not yet "caused it to rain upon the land," we see the allusion to the flood narratives in which the Lord "caused it to rain upon the earth." The reference to "no man to work the ground" (2:4b–5) points us to the time when the man and the woman would be cast from the garden "to work the ground" (3:23).

Thus, as an introduction to the account of man's creation, we are told that a "good" land had been prepared for him: "streams came up from the earth and watered the whole surface of the ground" (2:6). Yet in the description of that land, we can already see the time when man would become an alien and stranger in a foreign land.

MAN IN GOD'S IMAGE

Genesis 2 tells us that God fashioned the first man from the soil of the ground (2:7) and the woman from the side of the man (2:22). The narrative is quite clear that human beings have no biological antecedents. The first man was created from the ground. God fashioned his body and breathed into his nostrils the breath of life. The narrative is also quite clear that the first man and woman were essentially identical. God made them both in His image (1:27). When God made the woman, he did not have to breathe into her nostrils the breath of life because she was already alive from the life of the man. When she was brought to the man, he immediately recognized her as one like himself.

The way this story is recounted shows that its author understood it in realistic and literal terms. When God took one of the man's ribs from his side, He then "closed the flesh" over the place where He had taken the rib. That detail is not necessary to the sense of the story. It is necessary, however, for readers attempting to visualize God's actions in realistic and literal

Some scientists now insist that life could not have originated on this planet and thus must have been imported to earth in its complex form from another part of the solar system. Why are they making such statements? In order to retain the evolutionary theory of the origin of life.

It is now known that there simply was not enough time on a cooled-down earth for complex forms of life to have developed so early. Either life was created in a complex form, or life was imported to earth from somewhere else within our solar system where it had more time to develop. The most likely origin, say most astronomers, would be Mars.

There is a problem with Mars, however. There is no evidence that life ever existed there. Mars has been thoroughly scrutinized by scientists and has revealed no evidence of having ever supported even the basic conditions for life, let alone developed life itself. Moreover, it is unlikely in any theory of origins that life came from somewhere outside this planet.

That unlikelihood has now led some scientists to suggest that the evolutionary process was not as slow as was previously supposed. They say in a friendly environment like earth, early life forms would have flourished at a more rapid rate. Some scientists have even suggested that life itself could have developed — even into complex forms — literally overnight. According to one leading life scientist, Cyril Ponnamperuma at the University of Maryland, "once the conditions are right, it could happen in twenty-four hours."[1]

The late professor Ponnamperuma's reference to the possibility of complex forms of life developing "in twenty-four hours" invites comparison with the biblical account of the creation of life within a single twenty-four-hour day. Ponnamperuma didn't, of course, intend to confirm the biblical account. Nor does his statement confirm the biblical account. It does show, however, that the biblical account of creation is not inherently untrue merely because it teaches that life could originate within a small period of time. Ponnamperuma's remark at least shows that the biblical view is scientifically plausible.

On one of the most crucial questions of the relationship of Genesis 1 and science — the time period of the origin of life — the biblical account may be said to be eminently plausible. In fact, it is far more plausible than the reigning evolutionary theory of only a decade ago.

terms. The writer doesn't want us to think that God left the man to heal on his own. God, like a surgeon, repaired the wound before He went on to make the woman.

At first glance, the description of the creation of man in verse 7 is quite different from that of chapter 1. In chapter 2 man is made "from the dust of the ground" rather than "in the image of God" as in chapter 1. No two descriptions could be more distinct.

We should not overlook, however, that the topic of the "creation of man" in chapter 2 is not limited to verse 7. That subject is the focus of the whole chapter. What the author had stated as a simple fact in chapter 1 — mankind as male and female was created in God's likeness — is explained and developed throughout the narrative of chapter 2. We cannot contrast the creation of man in chapter 1 with only one verse in chapter 2; we must compare it to the whole chapter.

The author's first point is that man, though a special creature made in God's image, was still a creature like the others God had made. Man did not begin as a "heavenly creature." He was formed of the "dust of the ground." In light of the special treatment given to man's creation in chapter 1, this emphasis on man's "creatureliness" in chapter 2 is important. This narrative deliberately negates the notion that man's origin might be connected with the divine. Man's origin was from the dust of the ground — earth dust, not star dust.

One can also see in this picture of man's origin an anticipation of his destiny. After the Fall, mankind would again return to the "dust of the ground" (3:19). In creation, humanity arose out of the dust; in the Fall, he would return to that same dust. This graphically depicts the author's lesson on the contrast between the work of God and the work of man.

MALE AND FEMALE

In the first chapter, the author had intimated that man's creation in the "image of God" somehow entailed his creation as male and female: "In the image of God he created him; male and female he created them" (1:27). In chapter 2, the author has returned to develop that theme by showing that man's creation "in God's image" entailed a "partnership" with his wife. The "likeness" which the man and the woman share with God in chapter 1 finds an analogy in the "likeness" between the man and his wife in chapter 2. Here also, as in the first chapter, man's likeness to God is shown against the background of his distinction from the other creatures.

There can be no doubt that the author intended the account of the naming of the animals to be read as part of the story of the creation of the woman. This is made certain in verse 20 where, at the conclusion of the man's naming the animals, the author remarks, "but for man, he did not find a partner like himself." The author saw the man's naming the animals as a search for a suitable partner. In recounting that no suitable partner was found, the author has assured the reader that man was not like the other creatures. In contrast, the author records in graphic detail the words of the man when he discovered the woman: "This is now bone of my bone and flesh of my flesh…" (2:23). The man recognized his own likeness in the woman.

It is notable that upon first seeing his newly created wife, Adam speaks to her and even names her. He speaks a well-developed language, which implies he already had a culture and a world view which was reflected in that language.

By its sheer simplicity the biblical account leaves unanswered the questions that continue to baffle modern science. How did language and culture originate? How can language develop without a preexisting culture? How can there be a culture without a common language to hold it together? The Bible simply says that the man and woman enjoyed all these things from the very first. That is a big reason why the world God created for them could be considered so "good."

HOW DID WE GET WHERE WE ARE?

Genesis 1 and 2, understood within the broader context of the Pentateuch, paint a brilliant picture of the good land God prepared for the blessing of

His people. When these chapters are understood both as preparation for and a preview of the Sinai Covenant — the way I believe the author intended them to be understood — many of the troublesome questions that have vexed modern readers simply disappear.

This interpretation, while differing markedly from many contemporary views, is both faithful to the biblical text and connected to a long line of scholarly interpretations that span the centuries. In fact, before the rise of the modern scientific mind-set, the precursors to this view dominated the field.

If that is so, you might wonder why the situation changed. What happened to sweep away the older views in favor of those with a much more recent vintage? It is to those questions we turn in Part Four.

THE ROOTS OF THE PROBLEM

• Many valid observations about the sense of Genesis 1 and 2 are preserved in older, prescientific viewpoints. "New" is not always "better."

• Studying other views of Genesis 1 and 2 can help us understand more clearly our own interpretations.

• A little humility goes a long way in helping us understand Genesis 1 and 2.

• We must strive to be sensitive and alert readers of Scripture.

CHAPTER EIGHTEEN

IS NEWER ALWAYS BETTER?

ost of us have seen film clips of early attempts at powered flight. We have watched as inventors more courageous than wise mounted bicycles fitted with wooden wings. And we have laughed as their unwieldy inventions inevitably veered off their wobbly courses and collapsed in a heap of handlebars and splintered wing struts. When we compare such crude attempts with modern jet aircraft, of course we conclude that in technology and science, newer is better.

In fact, the cry "newer is better" has almost become our motto. In the twentieth century we have become used to the idea of progress and development. We take it for granted that modern views are better than older views. We wouldn't think of rejecting modern science in favor of an ancient superstition. Who would choose to ride horses and chariots rather than drive cars and fly in airplanes?

We tend to look at past views of the Bible in the same way, seeing older views as worn-out relics of outmoded times. We prefer modern views on the Bible, thinking they must be superior to earlier ones. After all, aren't they more recent? And newer is better!

Progress, however, is not measured the same way in biblical interpretation as it is in science and technology. In the interpretation of the Bible, the views of the past are as important as those of the present. The past still contains many valuable insights into the meaning of Genesis 1.

There is also no guarantee that current views are not fundamentally flawed. Contemporary issues and questions can distort our understanding of Scripture just as easily as they can help it. Much of our modern under-standing of the world and its problems has raised questions that have mis-directed our understanding of the Bible and left us blind to the concerns of the ancient author.

For that reason, observations from past interpreters often give us insights we might not have enjoyed otherwise. Earlier biblical scholars didn't face the same pressures that confront contemporary interpreters. While these older interpreters certainly had their own issues to contend with, they did not have ours. To view the text from their perspective can offer us a valuable and often revealing vantage point. That is why, in study-ing the Bible, we have to take time to look at the past seriously.

AGE DOESN'T MEAN ERROR

The truth or error of a biblical interpretation is not determined merely by its age. Ideas about the Bible — particularly Genesis 1 and 2 — have often been discarded, not because they were wrong, but because they no longer seemed to fit with modern ideas about the world. In fact, earlier interpre-tations of Genesis 1 were often discarded merely because they didn't address or answer modern questions.

But that is never a valid reason for rejecting an interpretation of the Bible. Interpretations, whether ancient or modern, must be evaluated by how well they enable us to explain the text. Do they help us understand what the text means? Or do they overlook important features of the text?

Studying various approaches to the opening chapters of Genesis — no matter how antiquated they may appear — is important to under-standing the Bible and its relationship to science. It is especially important for at least the following reasons.

WHY STUDY OLDER APPROACHES?

1. *A study of older approaches to Genesis 1 and 2 can point to the key pas-sages in these chapters.*

Through the centuries, the task of interpreting Genesis has repeatedly turned on the same basic questions. The text of these chapters has not changed, so the same textual questions persist today. Many solutions have been offered, both ancient and modern. By seeing how others have attempted to resolve the questions, we gain a clearer picture of the questions themselves — and may even discover the direction we should take to resolve them.

2. *A study of older approaches to Genesis 1 and 2 can help us avoid certain interpretive pitfalls.*

Rarely is a completely new interpretation offered for these chapters. In the seventeenth century, John Lightfoote, a noted Hebrew scholar, wrote a small commentary on Genesis that is full of helpful insights. Lightfoote recognized that many of his observations on Genesis would appear new and different, so he warned his readers in the title of his book. He called it *A few and new observations upon the book of Genesis. The most of them certain, the rest probable, all harmless, strange, and rarely heard of before.*[1]

Yet most, if not all, of Lightfoote's observations on Genesis already had been noted by the great medieval Jewish expositors of Scripture. Lightfoote's observations were not really "strange and rarely heard of before." He was certain, however, that his audience would find them so.

Whether we know it or not, most of our interpretations of Scripture have a long and complex history. Years of rigorous scrutiny and evaluation often reveal the strengths and weaknesses of the views. By studying the "life history" of older interpretations, we can see what caused them to develop and perhaps what caused them to fall.

Interpretations of such highly debated passages as Genesis 1 and 2 do not occur in a vacuum. They are often greatly influenced by outside cultural and intellectual forces. What were the issues of the day and age in which they arose? How did changing attitudes toward the Bible and science affect the interpretations of these chapters? We cannot afford to ignore these factors in our own interpretation of the Bible.

3. *A study of the history of the interpretation of Genesis can suggest approaches we might not otherwise have considered.*

Interpretation seeks to understand what a passage of Scripture is "about." What is the author saying? Often we may find it difficult to answer questions in our own words. Studying various interpretive approaches can give us new insights and categories to do that. Ultimately the process of interpretation involves "trying on an interpretation for size." Does it work? Does it help us understand the text? A good interpretation — and indeed the only valid one — is one which explains the text.

4. *Studying older views of Genesis 1 often helps us understand our own view more clearly.*

Most modern readers of the Bible have fairly definite ideas about the meaning of Genesis 1. They tend to think that everyone else views Genesis 1 and 2 in much the same way. Yet this doesn't mean they understand these chapters (nor even that they have actually read them!). In fact, what they "know" may be vague, tentative, and limited.

A study of the older approaches to Genesis 1 and 2 gives a clearer perspective of one's own view, as well as an awareness that not everyone who is on the side of the angels may agree with it.

5. *A study of older views of Genesis 1 can help reveal the impact of our own life situation on our reading of the text.*

Interpretations of passages like Genesis 1 and 2 are based on fundamental assumptions about the meaning of these passages — assumptions that have often gone unchallenged for centuries. We will probably never be able to isolate and identify all the assumptions we make when we read a text. It is important, however, to understand the general assumptions our own generation makes.

GAINING A BROAD PERSPECTIVE

Viewing the past gives an interpreter a broad perspective. We come to see ideas and viewpoints within the contexts that shaped them. The fact is, the Christian church has read Genesis 1 and 2 quite differently in various periods of its history. As our view of the world has become more scientific, we have tended to view these early chapters of Genesis within that expanded scientific world view.

At one time readers of the Bible had a very limited view of the world around them. During the Middle Ages, many believed that the world was small and flat and that the earth was the center of the universe. Without the tools and viewpoint of the modern world, they simply read the Bible within the context of their limited understanding. Such a perspective naturally influenced their understanding of Genesis.

As our understanding of the world changes, so does our understanding of Genesis 1. We inevitably force some of our own viewpoints on the world of the text. The result can be a fundamental distortion of the viewpoint of the Bible. In one sense there is little we can do about this. If we don't understand it from a familiar perspective, how can we understand it at all?

Let me give an example. I wear glasses. The prescription of my glasses is so strong that they often curve and distort my vision around the edges of the lenses. I have to recognize this and make adjustments when I use them. It's not a perfect solution, but what else can I do? I can't see at all without them. At the same time they help me see clearly, they also distort part of the world which they enable me to see.

The same is true when I attempt to understand the Genesis account of creation. I must read it from within a certain context and perspective. That very context, however, can distort the viewpoint of the text itself.

A study of the history of the interpretation of Genesis 1 can give us a sense of the limits and extent of our own perspective. We can see ourselves and our understanding of Genesis in light of how others before us have read it. When we look back at how others with quite different world views read these chapters, we can see more clearly how their contexts affected their interpretation. That awareness should make us sensitive to the same process at work in our own attempts to understand the text. Until we become sensitive to the role we play in determining the meaning of a passage like Genesis 1 and 2, we will not be able to look more clearly at the text itself.

IN SUMMARY: HEIRS TO A CLOUD OF WITNESSES

Any serious interpretation of Genesis 1 and 2 must reckon with the fact that our understanding of these chapters was not formed in a vacuum. We are all heirs to a great cloud of witnesses who have preceded us in reading these texts. Sometimes that cloud can block our vision of the text itself. At other times the testimony of past interpreters can block the bright light of the present issues from blinding our eyes to the actual meaning of the text.

We must learn to listen to those who have read these texts in bygone ages. We must learn to humbly acknowledge and accept the insight which comes from their perspective. Modern views of these chapters may be newer, but that does not mean they are better.

On the other hand, just because an interpretation is old doesn't mean it's right. Whether we realize it or not, many of our interpretations have been shaped by ancient ideas which long ago went out of favor. Yet these ideas continue to affect the way we read Genesis 1 and 2.

If we desire to gain a fresh understanding of what these biblical texts actually say, it is crucial that we understand how long-held beliefs about these texts still affect modern interpretations. In Part Four, therefore, we will turn our attention to some very old ideas that, even from the grave, continue to mold our understanding of the Bible's creation account.

• The biblical view of creation in Genesis 1 and 2 has rarely been left to speak for itself. It invariably gets squeezed into the mold of the prevailing world view.

• Those primarily responsible for reading the Bible through the lens of contemporary world views have, for the most part, been the Bible's own friends.

CHAPTER NINETEEN

FROM ONE WORLD TO THE NEXT

In a thought-provoking episode of *Star Trek: The Next Generation*, Lieutenant Commander Data, an android, crash-lands on a primitive planet and suffers amnesia. When members of the alien world's medieval population encounter him, Data can remember nothing — not where he came from, not his own unique nature, not even his name. Townspeople note his unusual appearance and guess he must be a traveler from across the distant mountains.

Unknown to the good citizens — and unremembered by Data — the damaged container the android carries is full of a dangerous, radioactive metal. The townspeople mistake the lethal substance for an attractive source of jewelry and begin making bracelets, necklaces, and other trinkets out of it. Soon they all start getting sick — except for Data.

As the story unfolds, Data recalls more and more of his training but nothing of his true origin. He sets up a crude laboratory to try to determine the cause of the epidemic but is opposed by the local "doctor" who is certain the malady comes from an imbalance of body fluids. The more science that Data remembers, the more convinced this "doctor" and her friends become that he must be an evil wizard. Eventually Data is attacked and killed (or, in his case, deactivated). Naturally, the intrepid crew of the Enterprise eventually tracks him down and manages to save him from cybernetic extinction.

The story portrays the cataclysm that can result when a more primitive world view collides with a newer one. And although this story is pure science fiction, the underlying theme has been played out in our own history more than once.

Perhaps you have already seen a similar conflict in this book. No doubt you have noticed that the conclusions drawn in *Genesis Unbound* differ markedly — sometimes radically — with contemporary interpretations which may be more familiar to many readers. Why is this so? Where do we get our understanding of these ancient texts? Why do we believe what we believe? These are the crucial questions I want to tackle now.

WHAT'S A COSMOLOGY?

A cosmology is an explanation or mental picture of the world. Throughout its long history, the Western world has attempted to visualize the nature and extent of the physical universe. The earliest of these cosmologies tried to discover the shape of the universe and the substance from which everything is made. People imagined the universe to be spherical and thought its primary substance was a sort of "basic matter" expressed in four elemental forms: earth, air, fire, and water. The whole of the universe was thought to consist of varying forms and mixtures of these basic elements.

Full-orbed descriptions of the universe soon developed from these early attempts. People drew mental pictures of the universe which became "cosmic maps" for finding their place within the world.

Primitive world views like these dominated the Western view of the universe for so long that invariably they found their way into our own thinking about the Bible. In fact, the story of the interpretation of Genesis 1 and 2 is often little more than the story of the relationship between the biblical view of creation and Western society's developing view of the world. Therefore, it is impossible to understand many current views of Genesis 1 and 2 without first grasping some very old views of the world.

THREE BASIC COSMOLOGIES

Three basic views of the world have dominated Western thinking over the past several thousand years: the Ptolemaic, Copernican, and Modern views. As each of these cosmologies rose to prominence, biblical interpretation sought to hold its own or face the charge of being irrelevant and outmoded. Therefore the important question for interpreters has always been, How does the biblical account square with the changing views of contemporary society? Unfortunately, that is a quite different question than simply, What is the meaning of the biblical account?

In attempting to answer the first question rather than the second, biblical interpretation has almost always taken the path of least resistance. Where it has found areas of similarity between the Bible and Western cosmologies, those areas have been emphasized to show the basic harmony between science and the Bible. Where there has been dissimilarity, those areas have been minimized.

Biblical interpretations developed during different eras of cosmological understanding show distinct differences in how they view Scripture. Therefore let's briefly review the three major cosmologies which have dominated Western thinking over the past centuries. In that way we will be better able to understand and appreciate specific biblical interpretations developed over that time.

THE PTOLEMAIC UNIVERSE

The ancient Greeks were the first to develop a full-scale picture of the universe. They viewed the world much as they viewed their own society. Both were considered well-organized, harmonious, basic units of nature. The Greek city, the *polis*, was thought of as an organized whole. Its people and its institutions all worked for the good of the city. In the same way, the world (or *cosmos*) was an organized whole. Its elements and its laws were aimed at producing the good, the beautiful, and the orderly.

The key concept in the Greek view of the world was *cosmos* — that which was "well-ordered" and "beautiful." It is the Greek term from which we get our English word "cosmetic." To the early Greeks, the world was a well-ordered, beautiful whole, aimed at producing the good. The opposite of *cosmos* was *chaos* — the world in total disarray. The word "chaos" in fact means that which is in "disarray" and "empty." The most basic form of the Greek view of origins taught that the cosmos arose out of a primeval chaos.

Over time the Greeks added many ideas to this basic notion of the universe as cosmos. Eventually it became widely accepted that the cosmos consisted of an organized system of spheres, each rotating around the same absolute center point. As this theory was finally perfected by the ancient astronomer Ptolemy (mid-second century A.D.), the earth was seen as the center of a complex, circular universe. Around the earth, in a series of ten spheres, rotated the sun, stars, and planets. The spheres of the sun and stars rotated from east to west, while the spheres of the planets rotated toward the east.

The relationship between the biblical account of creation in Genesis 1 and the Ptolemaic view of the universe seemed a perfect fit. Not that the Bible represented the Ptolemaic system — far from it! Yet both the Ptolemaic system and the Bible shared a similar focus: the earth.[1] So strong ties quickly developed between the biblical account and the Ptolemaic world view.

For the most part, those ties were not in the best interest of the Bible. The ease with which the biblical account could be related to the Ptolemaic system soon led to the virtual identification of the two systems. In the Middle Ages it was widely held that the biblical view of the world *was* the Ptolemaic view.

The Ptolemaic system dominated the Western world's view of the universe throughout ancient and medieval times until it was replaced (or at least highly modified) by the quite different view of Copernicus.

THE COPERNICAN UNIVERSE

Nicolaus Copernicus (1473–1543) turned the Greek, Ptolemaic universe on its head. He replaced the earth with the sun as the center of the cosmos. Though it seemed a small change, his view had a major effect on the popularly accepted view of the world. Now the universe appeared much larger, the stars much farther away, and the laws of nature much more complex than in the simpler Ptolemaic universe. As long as the sun, moon, and stars were thought of as circling the earth in their own orbits, the uniformity of the brightness of the stars had a ready explanation: They kept a steady distance from the earth.

If the earth circled the sun, however, then the earth must at times be closer to some stars than to others. But if that were true, why didn't the stars get brighter as the earth came closer to them? The answer had to be that the stars were much farther away than the Ptolemaic universe had supposed. The stars must, in fact, be enormously distant from the earth, which meant the universe had to be much larger than was ever imagined. Thus one of the most important changes brought by the Copernican world view was a growing appreciation for the enormous size of the universe.

In such a large universe, what held everything in place? According to the Ptolemaic system, the universe was held together by spheres which

---

WHAT ABOUT THE HOMINIDS?

Over the past century scientists have unearthed and studied the remains of non-human, but humanlike, creatures that science says inhabited the earth in a far distant age. At one time it was believed that these were remains of the immediate ancestors of human beings. Though many still hold that these creatures represent distant "relatives" of human beings, it is no longer possible to maintain they were related directly to modern humans.

We now know that the last of those creatures passed from the scene suddenly and without leaving any known descendants. Whatever kind of creatures they were, we can say with some confidence today that those creatures were not the immediate genetic ancestors of human beings. If their progeny were alive today, they would not be human beings. They disappeared without a trace, just as human beings appeared on the scene without a trace.

Today both science and the Bible agree that human beings did not descend from any known form of "pre-human" creatures. There was no "pre-Adamic" race of humans.

encircled the earth. Since in the Copernican system, the earth was no longer the center of the universe, new explanations about the "glue" were needed.

That glue was supplied by Isaac Newton's concept of gravity. Gravity held the universe together. No longer was there a discernible center to the universe — at least, the earth was not that center. Suddenly the earth appeared insignificant in light of the immense proportions the Copernican universe assumed.

For Christian theology and biblical interpretation, the "Copernican Revolution" had a far-reaching effect. Interpretations that had been accepted for centuries would have to be rethought and retooled. Yet one important part of the Greek world view did not change with Copernicus: the concept of a primeval chaos as the original state of the world. The notion that the universe arose out of a primeval mass of unformed material continued to lie behind the new views of the world spawned by Copernicus. This idea of a primeval chaos would even play an important role in later statements of science about the origins of the universe.

THE MODERN UNIVERSE

The Copernican view of the world did not stay static; it continued to be expanded by new discoveries even into the twentieth century. In time the universe was considered impossibly vast and filled with countless galaxies, dimensions, and other worlds.

With such an expanded universe, it became increasingly difficult to fit the biblical account of creation into that model — and even more challenging to fit such an expanded universe into the biblical account. By as early as the seventeenth century, attempts were made to adjust the biblical account to the size and scope of modern conceptions of the world.

Such attempts continue unabated to the present time. In a recent book on Genesis, the astrophysicist Dr. Hugh Ross has argued that the biblical account of creation parallels precisely the order of the formation of the universe as modern astronomers now understand it. Ross states that "today, thanks to the incredible information explosion of the past few decades...sufficient observational evidence has been gathered and analyzed to enable scientists to state conclusively how the universe and the solar system began and developed through time. This new set of theories, the first of its kind to be universally accepted among research scientists in various related fields of investigation, agrees in every point with the Genesis account as it is properly read and understood."[2]

The Creation Research Society, based in San Diego, California, also continues to argue that science — properly understood and practiced — agrees in whole and in part with the Bible. Creation scientists hold that Genesis 1 depicts the origin and formation of the pre-flood world. The earth was a veritable "hot house" of biological activity, enclosed in a gigantic water canopy, until the catastrophic flood of Noah put an end to those conditions and ushered in the world we now know. The biblical flood was so catastrophic in its effects on the earth that virtually all scientific evidence relating to the earth's origins was obliterated. What remains to be studied by geologists and scientists must be linked to the effects of Noah's flood.

Therefore, most creation scientists hold that little remains of the original earth created in Genesis 1 and 2. Science, they say, can tell us very little about that earth, and what it does attempt to say is based on the faulty theory of evolution. Thus they hold that the biblical account of creation is an equally valid, scientific picture of the earth's early ages.

HARMONIZING THE BIBLE WITH CULTURAL MODELS

The first, and perhaps most important, attempt to harmonize the biblical account of creation with an early cosmology is found in one of the Intertestamental books, The Wisdom of Solomon. That work was a self-conscious attempt to fit the biblical account of creation into the mold of the classic Greek cosmologies. It claimed the world was created "out of an amorphous mass,"[3] implying that matter is eternal. Therefore God's work of creation recorded in the Bible consisted only of forming the preexistent, unformed matter into the world which we now see around us.

The Wisdom of Solomon represents an early attempt to make the Bible conform to the Hellenistic world view.[4] It also shows that even before the time of Christ, the biblical view of creation had been made to conform to culturally acceptable ideas. What this early Jewish work attempted — and successfully achieved — was to be repeated countless times in subsequent centuries.

By contrast, it is clear the New Testament writers did not share completely the view of The Wisdom of Solomon. The writer of the book of Hebrews, for example, laid it down as a fundamental article of faith that the world was created out of nothing (*ex nihilo*).[5] Moreover, the prologue to John's Gospel states quite emphatically, "all things were made through him [the Word], and without him was not anything made that was made."[6]

Though the Church consistently rejected the idea that God created the world out of preexisting, unformed matter, it just as consistently retained the idea that the world was once a formless mass of chaos and that God shaped and fashioned it into the world which we know today. (We follow the development of that thought in a discussion of the "classic view" of creation in chapter 6). This idea of the unformed mass of creation, developed in The Wisdom of Solomon, has remained a part of the meaning of creation to this day.

WHAT'S THE EFFECT?

We are now ready to take a serious look at the impact which various non-biblical cosmologies have had on the understanding of Genesis 1 and 2 through the ages. How do such cosmologies continue to influence our understanding of Genesis to this very day? To fail to acknowledge this influence would be to abdicate our responsibility, as evangelical believers, to the text itself. It would also mean turning our backs on one of the most effective means for neutralizing the kind of distortion that outside interests often bring to the biblical text. What does the text itself say about God's creation of the world? That must always be our first interest.

• Western culture viewed the earth as the center of the universe. Most Christians also believed that is what Scripture taught.

• When modern science began to reshape its understanding of the world, the " biblical view" was often cast off as a part of an outmoded viewpoint.

• With the rise of independent scientific theories about the universe, the "biblical view" of creation became only one of many versions of the origin of the world.

• Until the rise of the theory of evolution, most scientific theories about the world were in essential harmony with the Bible.

• Modern evangelicalism maintains that both the Bible and science lead to the discovery of true knowledge about the world and its origin. *Genesis Unbound* seeks to explore the relationship between science and the Bible within the context of the meaning of the biblical text alone.

CHAPTER TWENTY

INTERPRETATION, THEN AND NOW

here and how do the many conflicting interpretations of Genesis 1 and 2 originate? Who thinks up all these interpretations? Was there ever a time when everyone who read the text understood it clearly and without problems? Were there great men from the past who wrote down the true meaning of books such as Genesis for us in later generations? Do we have such interpretations today? Why do we understand Genesis the way we do?

All these questions concern the history of interpretation. Go to any theological library, and you will find dozens of books on Genesis. There have been hundreds, even thousands, of books written on the interpretation of these early chapters. To prepare ourselves for our own investigation of these chapters, it will help to survey the major stages of the interpretation of Genesis 1 and 2 produced by Jewish and Christian scholars over the last two millennia. Every one of these stages has left its mark on the interpretive landscape.

PRE-CHRISTIAN JUDAISM (250 B.C. — A.D. 90)

In the pre-Christian era, Judaism embraced at least two distinct social and religious communities. On the one hand were the "Hellenistic" Jews who had been highly influenced by the Greek language and culture. On the other hand were Jewish communities that resisted outside influences and attempted to preserve the languages and culture of their forefathers. For lack of a better term, we can call such communities "Semitic."

Hellenistic interpretations of Genesis 1 and 2 are represented most clearly in the Greek translation of the Scriptures known as the Septuagint. While the origin of the Septuagint is shrouded in legend, we can safely say that it developed within the Greek-speaking Jewish community in Alexandria, Egypt, sometime before the last pre-Christian century (before 100 B.C.).

The Septuagint clearly attempts to harmonize the biblical account of creation with prevailing Greek views of the origin of the universe. At the time, several Greek cosmologies competed for acceptance, and the Septuagint translators appear to have chosen the one which they believed Genesis 1 and 2 most closely resembled — the view popularized in the Dialogs of Plato (specifically as it is represented in the Dialog known as Timaeos). There are good reasons to believe that the Greek translation of Genesis 1 and 2 once circulated within Jewish communities in pre-Christian times as a sort of Hellenistic Jewish tract which helped link the Bible and Greek culture.

Despite their strong desire to view Genesis 1 and 2 in light of early Greek cosmologies, the translators of the Septuagint were above all committed to rendering the Hebrew text accurately and faithfully. Their interpretations of Genesis 1 and 2 could therefore be introduced into their version only partially and in a widely diffuse manner. They intended to render Genesis in such a way that the biblical account could be thought to represent the early Greek view of the origin of the universe. The early Jewish Hellenists were so convinced that the Scriptures and the Greek philosophers held the same view of the world that they believed Plato and the other Greek philosophers of his day had read and studied the Pentateuch of Moses!

The views of the Greek-speaking, Jewish philosopher Philo (ca. 20 B.C. — A.D. 50) were a direct result of the successful merger of the Hebrew

Scriptures and Greek thought in the Septuagint. In turn, Philo's writings directly impacted early Jewish and Christian interpretation of the Old Testament.

Yet not all Jews in the pre-Christian era were intent on reading Genesis 1 and 2 in light of Greek cosmologies. Many Jewish scholars of that day were just as committed to reading the biblical creation account in light of the meanings they perceived within the Hebrew Scriptures themselves. Such interpreters wrote in Hebrew and Aramaic for Semitic-speaking Jews. The Book of Jubilees (ca. second century B.C.) is an example of one such attempt. It contains many insightful interpretations of Genesis 1 and 2 which have been largely overlooked or neglected in the Greek-dominated versions of creation. The views of these Hebrew-oriented Jewish scholars reappeared in later medieval Jewish commentaries.

EARLY CHURCH (A.D 90 — 750)

The Septuagint quickly became the Bible of the early Church. So it was natural that the Jewish interpreters who had worked most closely with the Septuagint had the greatest impact on the early Church. Philo is an important example. Through the work of the Christian biblical scholar Origen (ca. 185–254 A.D.), the views of Philo on Genesis 1 and 2 were the groundwork for nearly a millennium of Christian interpretation. Through Philo and Origen, the cosmology of Plato and the Pythagorean School continued to dominate the Christian interpretation of Genesis 1 and 2 for many centuries.

During this time, Jewish scholars also were busily studying their Hebrew Bibles. Much of their labors were carried out apart from the Septuagint. Their efforts show up most clearly in the early Aramaic Targums (translations) from Jewish communities in Palestine and Babylon. Although the Greek view of creation dominated the Christian interpretation of Genesis during this period, the influence of the Jewish Targums was also being felt. Many of the early, pre-Christian interpretations of the first chapters of Genesis were preserved by these Aramaic translations, which would later directly influence some Christian interpretations of Genesis.

Aristotelianism and its cosmological corollary, the Ptolemaic universe, dominated the interpretation of Genesis 1 and 2 in the medieval period. In Aristotelianism, the world was viewed as an enormous chain reaction of causes and effects. God was the First Cause, the Unmoved Mover who set into motion the whole of the cosmos. The universe was in constant motion, and every part of it maintained the motion given to it by the Creator. The movement of the physical world was thus understood as a natural consequence of its God-given nature. The sun, moon, and stars circled the earth in perfect spherical orbits because that was their nature.

Aristotelianism's effect on the interpretation of Genesis 1 and 2 was overwhelming, virtually identifying Genesis 1 and 2 with the Ptolemaic universe. Soon the idea of the Ptolemaic universe was raised to the level of infallible Church doctrine. To suggest that the Ptolemaic system was incorrect, or that it did not accurately represent the Genesis account, was to invite the charge of heresy. When in the early seventeenth century the Italian astronomer Galileo submitted proofs that Copernicus was correct — that the sun, not the earth, lies at the center of the solar system — he was forced to recant his views and was forbidden to teach. The stranglehold of Aristotelianism was broken only at the time of the Protestant Reformation when biblical exegesis was emancipated from Church tradition. Even then, the break was not immediate.

Meanwhile, Jewish study of the Hebrew Scriptures flourished. During the medieval period scholars renewed their focus on the study of Hebrew text, grammar, and words. Comprehensive and learned commentaries were written in Hebrew on virtually every aspect of the Hebrew Bible. Much of the work of these Hebrew scholars was carried out in isolation from the Greek-dominated Christian interpretations, though Jewish scholars were certainly aware of Christian views of the Old Testament. These medieval Jewish scholars would have a lasting effect on later Christian interpretation.

At the time of the Reformation, when Protestant theologians and scholars returned to the study of the Hebrew Bible and left many Church traditions, their only reliable guide to the meaning of the Hebrew Bible proved to be these medieval Jewish commentaries. Much of what we find in Luther's and Calvin's commentaries on Genesis can be traced directly to these medieval Jewish works. Their work remains today as a valuable source of commentary on the meaning of the Hebrew Scripture.

THE REFORMATION (A.D. 1492 — 1675)

A central tenet of the Protestant Reformation was that the Scriptures should provide their own interpretation; Scripture, rather than Church tradition, was the only valid interpreter of Scripture. In principle, this meant that the meaning of Genesis 1 and 2 was to be derived solely from the Scriptures themselves, quite apart from external, philosophical systems. In time, such a view proved to be a major force in undermining the authority of Aristotelianism and the Ptolemaic view of the universe. As other views of the nature of the universe arose, the biblical text was given increasing liberty to judge and assess those views.

The first step in loosening the centuries-long identification of the Ptolemaic universe with the biblical world view was marked by the 1543 publication of Copernicus's *Concerning the rotation of the heavenly worlds* (*De revolutionibus orbium caelestium*). In that work Copernicus sought to prove that the sun, not the earth, stood at the center of the solar system.

At first, Copernicus's views had little effect on how the Bible was read. Few biblical scholars (or scientists, for that matter) had the mathematical expertise to appreciate his theory. The weight of the evidence simply was not felt, so there was little compelling reason for questioning the Ptolemaic system. Church tradition had long identified the biblical view with the Ptolemaic view, and there was no reason to give it up.

When, on a rare occasion, Luther was confronted with Copernicus's theory, he was content to dismiss it with a reference to Joshua 10:12–13. There, he maintained, "Joshua commanded the sun to stand still, not the earth."[1] He inferred that the sun must therefore move around the earth, as Ptolemy had theorized. We should note that in this appeal to Joshua 10:13, Luther was being true to his Protestant principle. Rather than appealing to tradition to uphold the Ptolemaic view, he pointed to the Scriptures themselves (albeit, the Scriptures as seen through Ptolemy's grid!).

The fact that Luther and other reformers appeared to pay little attention to the views of Copernicus indicates that his radical views hadn't received sufficient notice to be considered a threat. It was some time before Copernicus's views were to upset the identification of Scripture with the Ptolemaic system. That time came when Galileo, with the help of the newly invented telescope, gave empirical evidence to support Copernicus's theory.[2] Galileo published his views in the work *Sidereus nuncius* in 1610, offering his conclusions to a broad, popular audience. His direct observations carried much weight with his readers (far more, for example, than Kepler's mathematical proofs).

Immediately the Catholic Church banned the reading or teaching of Copernicus's views. In 1616 the doctrine that the sun circled the earth was made an official tenet of the Church. Protestant theologians were in general agreement with such a position; they also believed the Scriptures represented the Ptolemaic world. Since they considered Ptolemy's system to represent the biblical view, they defended it in the cause of biblical truth. In their minds, to surrender the Ptolemaic world was tantamount to surrendering biblical truth itself.[3]

But the world was changing, forever. The seventeenth century witnessed a fundamental shift in the nature of scientific proof. By the middle of the century, the validity of mathematical proof and empirical evidence was everywhere acknowledged, and the new view of the world produced by the budding sciences gained widespread acceptance. The old Ptolemaic view of the world — with which the Bible had been identified — was quickly being replaced by a formidable rival, one that would achieve its full development under Sir Isaac Newton.

NEWTONIANISM (A.D 1675 — 1781)

Newton's theory of gravity, which explained how the universe could hold itself together, marked a fundamental transition in the relationship between science and the Bible. The debate between the Ptolemaic and the Copernican universe had been largely an intramural scuffle about the locations of the earth and the sun. Traditional views of Genesis 1 and 2 continued to fit nicely within the confines of either system. Problems largely focused on the proper way to expound the meaning of the text. The scientific view of the world largely followed the exposition of Genesis 1 and 2. There was not yet a rival scientific world view developed extra-biblically through direct observation of nature.

With Newton, however, the universe suddenly became large — enormous, in fact. So gargantuan was Newton's universe that it threatened to burst the seams of the traditional view of Genesis 1 and 2. Newton's universe contained the seeds of a new world.

The century which followed Newton was a time of exploration and experimentation, not only of the physical universe but also of the relationship of the universe to the world depicted in the early chapters of Genesis. Theologians and biblical scholars responded to the changing views of science in two distinct ways:

1. Some continued to hold dogmatically to a pre-Newtonian view of the universe.

2. Others constructed bold and comprehensive new views of the relationship between science and the Bible.

Virtually every view of Genesis 1 and 2 current today was forged and developed during the century which followed Newton.[4] Each of these views presented itself to the scientific community as a serious attempt to describe the world of the Bible and the origin of the universe. Each view was critiqued and evaluated based on the growing data about the nature of the universe and on the basis of sound exegetical and historical procedures. One historian has described this century as a period of natural-theological dogmatism.[5] Dogmatic tenets from Scripture were melded with those from the observations of nature into comprehensive explanations of the origin and nature of the universe. During this whole period, the views of science and the views of Scripture were held in essential harmony. But already the biblical account was some the worse for the effort.

NATURALISM (A.D 1781 — 1877)

In the late eighteenth and early nineteenth centuries science separated from religion as a distinct field of knowledge. During this time individual scientific disciplines such as astronomy, geology, and biology developed into individual branches of learning. Observation and experimentation became the accepted sources of knowledge, while the Scriptures were discounted as a serious tool for learning about the physical world. If the biblical world was to be correlated with the scientific view of the world, the two would first have to stand on their own. Scientific inquiry could not be guided by Scripture.

In many ways this period was the reverse of the one which preceded it. In the early eighteenth century, the Bible held the key to knowledge about the nature of the physical world; scientists read their Bibles and accepted the world depicted in it, even incorporating its narratives into their scientific explanations of the physical universe. But by the late eighteenth century, scientific knowledge became the primary source for understanding the nature of the biblical world. What was learned about the world from science was taken as an explanation of what the Bible was about. The "days" of Genesis 1, for example, were identified as geological ages.

Though scientific knowledge developed independently of the scriptural text, still a general harmony existed between science and the Bible. The results of science were often seen as a source of "natural revelation" of God's glory in creation. The God of the Bible and the God of creation were one. God had revealed His truth in both nature and the Bible.

All that changed, however, with the publication of Darwin's *Origin of the Species* in 1859.

DARWINIANISM (A.D. 1859 — 1914)

In the Darwinian view of the world, no place remained for central biblical concepts such as creation, purpose, design, and destiny. All were replaced by the single notion of natural selection. What previous generations of scientists had seen as evidence of God's glory in creation, Darwin saw as the operation of a simple, primal force: the will to survive.

With the advent of Darwinianism, little hope endured to maintain a friendly relationship between science and the Bible. Instead, conflict and suspicion arose, and the scientific view of the world was cast as an alternative to the biblical view. The Bible and science went their separate ways. Science was given the task of constructing our knowledge of the world, while the Bible and theology were given the task of supporting our faith.

EINSTEIN (RELATIVISM)

The publication of Albert Einstein's general theory of relativity in 1915 did not inaugurate a new era in the relationship of science and the Bible, but it did fundamentally affect our understanding of the nature of scientific knowledge. Whereas throughout the nineteenth century scientists had become accustomed to viewing the biblical world view as encased in ancient, "pre-modern" categories and social forms, they had continued to think of scientific knowledge as objective and absolute. In the minds of most scientists and scholars, the biblical understanding of the world was true only within a limited context and only when understood as an accommodation to ancient ways of thinking. Scientific knowledge, on the other hand, was thought to be true and objective in an absolute sense.

Einstein's general theory of relativity changed all that. Einstein had demonstrated that even the most fundamental principles of natural science — such as the nature of time and space — were not objectively true. They were true only under certain circumstances and within a limited frame of reference. Scientific knowledge thus came to be understood as relative, subject to certain conditions and to the same contextual limitations as the Bible. Scientific knowledge itself was a form of accommodation.

In the twentieth century we have gradually come to recognize that forms of knowledge which come from non-scientific sources (such as the Bible) can, if properly understood, have just as much value as rigorous forms of scientific knowledge. *All* knowledge is relative, be it biblical or scientific. All knowledge is a form of accommodation and must be interpreted within its appropriate context.

EVANGELICALISM

Not all modern theologians and biblical scholars have accepted the verdict of the relativity of biblical knowledge. Classical evangelicalism, for example, has continued to maintain that biblical truth corresponds to reality in the same way as does scientific truth. Though there are areas of knowledge where relativity applies — nuclear physics, for example — scientific knowledge based on simple observations of the world and experimentation is also true knowledge.

In other words, evangelical theologians have preserved the basic tenet of the Genesis creation account that God created the world and that He made men and women an essential part of it. What we see and understand about the world is true knowledge because we, as human beings, are created in God's image.

What has this meant for evangelicalism? While most other forms of Christian theology (Roman Catholicism and liberal Protestantism, for example) have made a separate peace with modern scientific theories of origins, an ongoing debate has continued within evangelicalism over the relationship of science and the Bible. That debate has centered on three distinct areas.

1. Evangelicalism has continued to resist the underlying assumptions of Darwinian evolution. In some cases (Scientific Creationism, for example), evangelicals have sought to build their own alternative scientific explana-

tion of such central features of modern evolutionary theory as the fossil record, the geological ages, and the age of the universe.

2. Evangelicalism has continued to look for areas within the modern scientific consensus which either correspond to or correlate with the biblical view of creation.

3. Evangelicalism has continued to find clues within the biblical text itself as to the nature of creation and the meaning of Genesis 1 and 2. In that regard, evangelicalism has followed the lead of the earliest reformers and the biblical writers themselves. They have allowed Scripture, not science, to interpret the meaning of Scripture.

In this book I have been attempting to address the larger question of the Bible and science by focusing specifically on this third concern. The biblical text itself has been our constant focus. What are the internal clues to its meaning? What is the biblical author attempting to say?

It is only from that perspective that evangelicalism can hope to forge a viable view of the relationship of science and the Bible.

• Translations of the Bible, particularly the King James Version, have had an enormous influence on how we understand the Genesis creation account.

• One of the most prevalent models of creation fostered by English translations of the Bible is the "primeval chaos" view. This view causes most conflicts with modern scientific theories.

• The main problem with the "primeval chaos" view of Genesis 1 is that it effectively conceals many of the real questions posed by the creation account. Without truly sensing the questions raised by Genesis 1, the reader is in no position to understand it.

CHAPTER TWENTY-ONE

THE KING JAMES LIVES ON

O ne problem which markedly affects our understanding of Genesis 1 is that we read the Bible in an English translation. Few contemporary readers study the Bible in the original Hebrew. Although there is nothing inherently wrong with English translations, they represent the end product of a good deal of thought about the meaning of these texts. Behind our translations lie many assumptions and interpretations. Not knowing what those assumptions and interpretations are can greatly restrict the range of meaning which these texts convey to us.

While English versions of the Bible agree on many of the fundamental issues in Genesis 1, the fact that they agree doesn't mean they are correct. It may simply mean our English translators have generally followed a uniform tradition. That tradition often reflects the interpretation of the earliest English translations.

AN EXAMPLE FROM 1611

The King James Version of the Bible, for example, has had an extraordinary influence on the way we read the Scriptures today. Fortunately, the King James Version is an excellent translation produced by scholars of great distinction. Yet they often merely followed their predecessors on fundamental issues. One such issue is the meaning of the term which is translated "earth" (which we looked at closely in chapter 4).

The appearance of the word "earth" in the King James translation of Genesis 1:2 gives the typical English reader the impression that the events in that chapter are about our whole world. In today's English, "earth" usually refers to our planet. At the time the King James Version was printed, the English word "earth" could also mean "land" in a local sense — the soil which was available for planting crops, the dry ground (as opposed to the sea). Even today we speak of bulldozers as "earth movers."

While the Hebrew word in 1:2 can mean "earth" in the modern sense, in the Bible it more often means the "land" where human beings dwell. Throughout Genesis and the Pentateuch, the term "land" most often refers to the land which God promised to give the sons of Abraham in fulfillment of His covenant in Genesis 15:18. In that verse we learn that God did not promise to give Abraham and his descendants the planet "earth," but rather a specific locality, the "land."

In Hebrew the same word can be used for both ideas. It is up to the translators to decide which English word best describes the intent of a particular passage.

Having taught Hebrew to seminary students for many years, I know how easy it is for one's understanding of the English text to dictate the meaning of the Hebrew text. Invariably in translating familiar passages, students will render a verse or a sentence just as the King James Version has it. They aren't wrong in their translation. What they fail to see, however, is that suddenly, at the end of the twentieth century, they have begun to speak like a seventeenth century Englishman!

The task of translating a book like the Bible into another language involves more than finding the right words. Translation involves an interchange of meaning, both at the level of the individual words and at a higher level, the level of a whole text. Since language is the primary tool by which human beings express their view of the world, translation often involves moving between quite different views of the world.

THE SEPTUAGINT

The early Jewish translators of the Bible certainly were required to move between quite different views of the world. As we have seen, when they rendered the Hebrew Book of Genesis into Greek, they went to great lengths to ensure it fit well into Greek ways of thinking.

The translators set out to show that the Book of Genesis presented precisely the same view of creation as the Greek world view. The world began as chaos — "invisible and unfurnished" as the Greek translation put it in Genesis 1:2 — and was completed as an organized and harmonious "cosmos." Thus the Septuagint closed its account of creation by rendering Genesis 2:1, "Now the heaven and earth were completed as a perfect *cosmos*." The biblical account was shown to conform to the Greek concept of creation.

For the next thousand years, the Jewish and Christian understanding of the Genesis account was fundamentally shaped by this Greek translation. The Septuagint was the Bible of the early Church, and it was a major part of the Church during the Middle Ages. The Latin Bible, the Vulgate, was itself a translation fundamentally shaped by the Greek Bible. Thus in an early period, concepts about creation which had been borrowed from the Greeks made deep inroads into both the Jewish and Christian understanding of the Bible. It became difficult, if not impossible, to read the opening chapters of Genesis apart from the influence of the Greek Bible and the Greek cosmologies.

REFORMATION TRANSLATIONS

At the time of the Reformation, the Protestant Church largely freed itself from its dependency on the Greek and Latin translations of the Bible and returned to a serious study of the original Hebrew. By that time, however, the interpretation of Genesis 1 and 2 in the Greek Bible had already become a lasting part of the Church's tradition — and it was to remain an essential part of that tradition for centuries to come. Even in the works of the great Reformers and exegetes (Luther and Calvin, for example), there was little fundamental questioning of the old view. Although these men were highly skilled Hebrew scholars, for the most part, the Hebrew text was interpreted in light of the creation traditions which had been established by the Greek Bible.

When did life begin on this planet, and what process of development did it undergo? Does the fossil record reflect the development of life on earth? Did simple forms of life develop into more complex forms and eventually into human life as we know it today? These questions are raised not only by biblical creationists today. Though modern scientists are not likely to accept the creationists' interpretations of Genesis 1, they do agree that classical theories such as Darwinian evolution need serious reassessment.

In classical evolutionary theory, life began spontaneously on this planet millions, or even billions, of years ago. It began in simple forms and evolved gradually into more complex forms, eventually reaching the higher forms of animal and human life. Long periods of time were assumed because of the complexity of life itself and the necessity of billions of trial and error attempts before that complexity would evolve. When the classical theories of evolution were being formulated, there seemed to be no limits on the amount of time one could allow for the formation of life on earth.

With new methods of research, however, problems have arisen in the classical model. For one thing, the amount of time for life to develop on earth has become impossibly small. By most geological reckonings, the earth is about 4.5 billion years old. We are told that the earth was extremely hot in its initial stages and continued so for millions of years. Throughout this period, the earth was repeatedly bombarded by asteroids from outer space. The thousands of craters on the surface of the moon are vivid reminders of the intensity of bombardment of the earth and the moon during that time.

Such massive impacts would naturally add heat to the earth's overall temperature. The continuous bombardments of the earth would impact its temperature in the same way as the burner on a stove keeps a boiling pot hot. The earth could begin to cool only after the asteroids ceased to rain upon it. Evidence suggests the earth could not have cooled sufficiently for life to exist until about 3.8 billion years ago.[1] After that point, and no earlier, life could have originated and begun its long development down to the present.

At rates commonly agreed on by biologists, it is usually held that 3.8 billion years could theoretically accommodate such a process. There was sufficient time for the chance creation of highly simplified forms of life. There was, however, not much time to spare.

In recent years an even greater problem has arisen — one that makes it virtually impossible to conceive of life forming on this planet within the framework of classical evolution theory. As new techniques have given us a closer look at the earliest stages of life on this planet, microscopic examinations of the earliest rock formations have revealed the presence of highly complex microscopic fossils. Those fossils have been found embedded in rock formations dated almost 3.5 billion years old. In other words, just after the earth had cooled sufficiently to support any form of life, complex microorganisms began to show up. So far, fossils of those microorganisms represent eleven species in five different genera.[2]

What is important about these early forms of life is that their biological life support systems were virtually the same as those of modern forms of life. That means they lived in the same way and by the same processes as life on earth today. For all intents and purposes, they were modern forms of life.

Though it may seem a long time by our standards, the few hundred million years between the time the earth cooled (3.8 billion years ago) and the existence of these complex forms of life (3.5 billion years ago) is far too short a period to support modern scientific explanations of the origin of life on earth.

Luther, whose commentary on Genesis showed many signs of original thinking, did not depart from the idea of a primeval chaos in Genesis 1. On Genesis 1:1, Luther wrote, "It says 'heaven and earth' not in the sense that they are now (in their finished form), but rather that which is in its rude and unformed state."[1] Calvin followed the same line of interpretation. About Genesis 1:1, he said, "Simply put, Moses intends to say that the world was not perfect at its very beginning, as we now see it, but that it was created to be an empty chaos of heaven and earth."[2] Though both Luther and Calvin discussed the Hebrew text at length in their commentaries, they never veered from the notions of a primeval "chaos" which the Greek translators attached to that text. They assumed the idea of a primeval chaos was contained in their Hebrew text.

This was not the first time, nor the last, that the meaning of the Hebrew text was made to conform to the prevailing world view.

To this day, the King James translation is the most memorable English version in existence, and it continues to influence virtually all modern translations. The King James rendered Genesis 1:2, "And the earth was without form, and void...." The terms "without form, and void" were the translators' way of describing their belief in the primeval "unformed mass."

According to the King James, the "heaven and earth" which God created "in the beginning" was not the "heaven and earth" we now know. It was, rather, the unformed mass that was to become the "heaven and earth" we see around us today. The "heavens and earth" were merely the material from which the world was to be made. The second verse is thus rendered "without form, and void" to show that the "heaven and earth" in verse 1 was unformed matter.

It's like when someone builds a house. The lumber company drops off a large pile of wood on the lot. That wood is the material from which the house will be built. It consists of two-by-fours, four-by-fours, and an assortment of other lumber. The owner of the house may look at the pile of wood and say, "That's my house." What he means is that it is the material from which his house will be built.

In taking that line of interpretation, the King James translators followed a pattern already established in the earlier English translations. The Geneva Bible, for example — which had also rendered verse 2 as "without form and void" — explained the phrase in their marginal notes as "a rude lump."[3] William Tyndale (1530) rendered the phrase as "void and empty."[4] Those translations, in turn, had taken their lead from the Latin Vulgate, which had rendered the expression as "empty and void."[5]

While it is probably safe to say that few people today understand the terms "formless and void" in the way these early translations intended them, it is important to recognize that translations such as the King James Bible reflected very definite ideas about the meaning of these biblical texts. Those translators were clear about their desire to express the idea of "unformed mass" by the terms "formless and void." We know this not only from the sense of the text as they rendered it but also from their commentaries on Genesis 1.

Whether or not the Hebrew words in this verse actually mean "formless and void" (see chapter 5), the King James translators believed they did. And today, we read Genesis 1 in English translations that largely follow the lead of the King James. Although the Bibles use more contemporary English, the meaning they convey has remained essentially the same.

RECENT VIEWS

The "primeval chaos" view has continued to play a major part in the translation and interpretation of Genesis 1. In one way or another it has helped shape every major view of biblical creation. One reason for its strong and lasting appeal is that for hundreds of years it linked the Genesis account to a general view of the world that seemed credible at the time. That very strength, however, has also proved a great liability. What happens to the biblical view of creation when the Greek view is no longer accepted?

With the rise of new scientific world views, ancient Greek concepts of the universe (including that of a primeval chaos) were largely set aside in favor of the ideas of Newton and Einstein. Neither Newton's nor Einstein's universe posited an early chaos out of which order arose. For both scientists, the laws of nature were eternal and, within specific contexts, inviolable.

Because the biblical view of creation has been linked so closely with the outmoded Greek view, the biblical view has often been dismissed. Many attempts to relate the biblical view of creation in Genesis 1 with that of "modern science" have in reality been attempts to come to terms with the Greek concept of "primeval chaos."

The "gap theory," for instance, was devised specifically to deal with the question of how a good God could create a "world in chaos." The "gap theory" posited that the "chaos" of Genesis 1:2 was not the original state of the world, but rather was the result of a wholesale destruction of the earth by Satan. Gap theorists never questioned the notion of a primeval state of "chaos" in Genesis 1; on the contrary, that idea forms the basis of the theory.

The primeval chaos view has proved in another way to be a liability to understanding Genesis 1: It has effectively walled off further serious reflection on the meaning of the Hebrew text. Rarely do translations or commentaries question the precise meaning of the terms rendered "formless and void," outside the context of primeval chaos. Rarely have biblical scholars asked, in any fundamentally new way, What is the meaning of the Hebrew terms *tohu wabohu* in Genesis 1:2? For the most part, Christian scholarship has been content to ask only how the earth became the chaotic mass we supposedly find in Genesis 1:2.

Recently, however, that situation has begun to change. There is now an increasing concern to explore the sense of the Hebrew terms *tohu wabohu* outside the context of primeval chaos. To that extent, we can say that biblical scholarship has begun to rediscover the sense of Genesis as it was understood by the Jewish scholars who long ago looked elsewhere than to the early Greek translations for the meaning of those terms.

The Jewish biblical scholars who focused their study on the Hebrew text were quite opposed to the notion of God's creating unformed chaos. Medieval Jewish commentaries, for example, maintained that the "heavens and earth" in Genesis 1:1 referred to the sky above and the land below. They were not "formless and void" but rather "an empty wasteland, devoid of plants, animals, and human beings."[6] Ibn Ezra (1092–1167), the renown Jewish expositor of Scripture, understood "the heavens and earth" in Genesis 1 to be "the firmament and the dry land," just as they are called within the first chapter. Ibn Ezra understood the phrase "without form and void" to mean "the land" was uninhabited because it was covered with water, not that the earth was formless chaos.[7]

Rashi saw no "unformed mass" created on the first day, either. According to him, "[the lights] had been created on the first day, but on the fourth day God commanded them to be suspended in the firmament. Indeed, all the productions of heaven and earth were created on the first day, but each of them was put in its place on that day when it was so commanded."[8] The "heavens and earth" consisted of all the unassembled parts of the universe. The world was created as a sort of prefabricated house. All the pieces — the heavenly bodies — were created on the first day and were made ready to be put in place. On the fourth day, the parts were assembled and the stars hung in their places.

Some Christian expositors have followed this line of Jewish interpretation, but not many. We already mentioned John Lightfoote, a Christian scholar highly skilled in Hebrew and in the study of Jewish commentary. Lightfoote followed Ibn Ezra's interpretation of "formless and void." According to Lightfoote, the land was "uninhabitable" because it was covered with water and had not yet been planted with foliage.

One of the most influential commentaries in the nineteenth and twentieth century, that of C. F. Keil, takes the precise view of Rashi: "After the general statement in ver. 1 as to the creation of the heavens, all that is mentioned is their completion on the fourth day, when for the first time they assumed, or were placed in, such a position with regard to the earth as to influence its development."[9]

Another variation states that the original "heavens and earth," created on the first day, was extended by God's creation of the "expanse" on the second day. Thus on the fourth day, the (primeval) light created on the first day had to be dispersed throughout the larger universe by means of "light sources," such as the sun, moon, and stars.[10]

IN SUMMARY: MODERN TRANSLATIONS AND OLD BELIEFS

It is crucial to remember that the primeval chaos view was reflected in some of the earliest translations of the Bible and continues to find its way into modern English translations. One reason for its lasting influence is the role it has played in resolving some of the central internal questions raised by the biblical account. When viewed closely, the creation account in Genesis 1 contains truly knotty, interpretive problems. Many who set out to resolve those problems found the concept of a primeval chaos to be a helpful tool. There has thus accrued a substantial apologetical investment in the idea of a primeval chaos. That investment has not been easy to part with. Like a bad habit, it's hard to kick because it does serve a useful function. The problem is that the function it serves, though good in itself, ultimately hinders our understanding of the creation account.

We cannot rest solely on the decisions of early translators. We must look at the original Hebrew text and, to the best of our abilities, follow the sense of the passage as it was likely understood by its first recipients. After all, the Hebrew text — not the English translations — is the inspired Word of God.

ON TO THE CLASSIC VIEW

Our understanding of Genesis 1 and 2 today has been largely shaped by certain basic and widespread views about the meaning of that text. The sum of those views I have chosen to call the "classic view." It is nearly impossible for English readers of the Bible to escape the impact of that view. Therefore let's take a closer look at the "classic view" to better appreciate the strengths of the alternative view of Genesis 1 and 2 presented in this book.

IN BRIEF

• A standard set of assumptions about the meaning of Genesis 1 can be thought of as the "classic view." We must ask whether those assumptions are actually taught in the Bible or are added by interpreters.

• The "classic view" contains many valuable insights into the original author's meaning. Yet it must be tested according to the statements of the text itself.

CHAPTER TWENTY-TWO

THE CLASSIC VIEW

A n international student of mine once told me that when he first came to America, he had a very difficult time adjusting to the everyday customs of meeting and greeting people. When his newly acquired American friends greeted him, they waved their hands in a way that, unbeknownst to them, meant "good-bye" to him. They assumed their hand motions were universally understood to mean "Hello! Come over here," when, in fact, my international friend understood them to mean, "Good-bye! See you later."

How often we are unaware that even simple patterns of meaning can greatly affect our day-to-day living. That is true in biblical interpretation, as well.

FIVE CORE ASSUMPTIONS

Many people read Genesis 1 and 2 without realizing that certain core beliefs lie behind some of our most widely used English translations of the Bible. These core beliefs have been particularly resistant to change, especially those that lie deep beneath the surface of the text. Many times these beliefs involve the meaning of a word here and a word there, as well as a basic assumption about the sense of the whole account.

It is that basic core — the "classic view" — which we will examine in this chapter. The classic view is not so much a specific interpretation of Genesis 1 as it is a set of at least five basic assumptions about it. Although the classic view evolved greatly in response to changing views of the world, the basic core remained firm.

It is thus important to ask whether such underlying assumptions about the meaning of Genesis 1 are "biblical." Do these assumptions square with the sense of the text? Are they what the original author intended? We have to take a hard look at these basic assumptions and be prepared to replace them, if necessary, with more appropriate core beliefs about the text.

1. The phrase "heavens and earth" in 1:1 refers to a primeval mass of unformed material from which God made the universe. That unformed mass is called "chaos."

Perhaps the most basic assumption is that Genesis 1:1 describes God's creation of an "unformed mass" of material best described as "chaos." God, like any wise builder, first gathered the material He would need for His work, then made the world from that material. Unlike a human builder, however, God did not gather His material from existing rocks and boulders. When God began His work, there were no rocks and boulders; there was nothing. God created the material in Genesis 1:1. He then made the world from that material, as recorded in the rest of the chapter (Genesis 1:2–31).

Early commentaries on Genesis contain endless discussions about the exact makeup of this "unformed mass." Was it primarily water? Was it a mixture of the basic elements — fire, water, air, and dirt? If so, How did fire mix with water? Eventually it was agreed that this primeval mass was something like a huge pile of mud. From this blob of unformed matter, God made the earth, the waters, the heavens, and eventually all living creatures, including human beings.[1]

In time, this view of Genesis 1:1 became so widely accepted that expositors saw no need to explain it; it was simply assumed. Unchallenged, the view became even more meaningful and influential.

This view is the foundation of virtually every interpretation of Genesis 1:1 from earliest times down to our own day. The average reader today may be unaware of this view, but it is deeply rooted in biblical interpretation (though it is rarely acknowledged). Silently and powerfully it continues to influence the central lines of interpretation of the first verse of the Bible.

I bought a new home last summer, which faces the northwest and sits forty or fifty feet from the road. That road takes me to a county highway, and that highway leads to an interstate. Why is my house sitting where it is? Why does the road leading by my house take the turns that it does? Why did they put the interstate highway four miles from my house, rather than two?

The simple answer is that my house sits on a lot that was measured to fit with a road built to take me to a county highway. Those measurements were carefully drawn according to long-established boundary markers.

My lot was drawn only a few decades ago, but it was measured according to markers that were laid out, in some cases, hundreds of years ago. Only an experienced surveyor would be able to uncover those ancient boundary markers today. Those markers, however, still continue to influence my life in many ways. They determine how early I must get up in the morning to go to work, how often I must paint my house, and where I walk my dog (to mention only a few). I may not think much about why and how those early boundaries were laid down, but they nonetheless continue to influence my daily life.

Our cities and highways were built to accommodate a way of life that is quickly passing away. The road going by my house which takes me to a highway leading into the city was ultimately built to get me to work and home again every day. Anyone familiar with the transportation systems of large, modern cities (such as Los Angeles) knows what is happening now to that ideal. Fortunately, just when we need it most, the electronic revolution is making it possible to live hundreds, or thousands, of miles from one's daily workplace. I can live in Montana and work for a company in Chicago if I want to. The road going by the house in Montana doesn't have to go anywhere except to a post office or an airport. That road, however —

if and when it is ever built — will surely be drawn according to those early boundary markers laid down in the days when the universal means of getting to work was the horse.

In the same way, much has changed in our understanding of the world since the earliest translations of the Bible. No one today believes the universe was originally a lump of mud waiting to be fashioned and formed into the earth and the stars. Nevertheless, we still read this passage as it was translated by and for people who *did* believe precisely that. Our new translations do not differ significantly on this basic point from the older versions; therefore our understanding of Genesis 1 is heavily influenced by an understanding of the text that comes from a much earlier and different age.

We have poured new wine into old wineskins. That sometimes creates serious difficulties and often requires a reassessment of some of the basic tenets which underlie our modern translations.

2. The creation of "light" on the first day refers to a special and unique light which divided the day and night before God created the sun on the fourth day.

One does not have to read much of the studies of Genesis 1 to discover the problem posed by God's command in verse 3, "Let there be light." How can there be light on the first day when the sun, moon, and stars do not seem to be created until the fourth day?

This question was resolved in the classic view by assuming that on the first day God created a unique, temporary form of light without a light source. Because the light had no source, it was not limited to a particular location and hence could travel in any direction — even around the earth to produce "day and night." We must remember that earlier biblical interpreters did not understand the nature of light as we do today. They could assume that light could travel in a circle.

Over the years many details were added, but the basic idea remained the same. As His first act of shaping and forming the primeval chaos into the world we now know, God created light. This temporary, primeval light made it possible to divide the first three days into "day and night." The primeval light circled the unformed mass of earth and marked the light and darkness. With the creation of the sun, moon, and stars on the fourth day, this primeval light was gathered into the newly formed sun where it still resides.

Luther says of Genesis 1:3, "Here an often repeated question arises, What kind of light was this which illumined the crude mass of heaven and earth? Though the sun and stars were not yet created, the text clearly shows that this was real physical light."[2] Yet it was a light which divided day and night until the sun was created. Thus Luther went on to ask the natural question, "Does this light move itself in a circular motion?"[3] Though he professed not to know from the narrative itself, Luther went on to give his own view: "If anyone, however, desires to know what to me seems most likely, I think the light was mobile so that the light made a natural day by rising in the east and setting in the west."[4] Luther confessed that the exact nature of this light "is difficult to say,"[5] but he argued that we must not depart from the clear and simple sense of the text. "Moses distinctly says 'there was light,' and he counts this as the first day of creation."[6]

Though to modern ears such an explanation sounds farfetched, it must be viewed against the prevailing alternative view in Luther's day that the "light" in 1:3 referred to the creation of angels. Thus when God separated "light" from "darkness" He was separating the good angels from the bad. The idea that this "light" was actually a physical light formed a major part of Luther's serious attempt to read the Genesis account "literally." If the text said, "And there was light" on the first day, and if the text also said the sun was created on the fourth day, then the light of the first day must not be sunlight, but another form of light without a source. Moreover, if the text said that the first day was marked off by a "day and night," then this light must have had a beginning and an end. Since by most reckonings of Genesis 1 in Luther's day the earth was not yet rotating — or, at least, not rotating with any regularity (it was in chaos) — the light itself must have moved around the formless earth.

In his commentary, Calvin made the point that God created the light before the sun and other heavenly bodies for a distinct purpose: to show that God, and not the sun and stars, was the ultimate source of all light.[7] Moreover, the primeval light alternated with darkness to produce day and night during the first week of creation.

Both Luther and Calvin appear to have relied on a widespread Jewish interpretation of Genesis 1. The medieval Jewish biblical scholar Rashi, for example, held that during the first three (or all seven) days of creation a "primeval light and darkness functioned together as day and night." After the creation of the sun, however, that light was stored away for the enjoyment of the righteous in the future.[8]

3. The sun, moon, and stars were created on the fourth day.

The question of exactly what happened on the fourth day of creation has long puzzled biblical commentators. On the face of it, the text appears clear enough: "And God said, 'Let there be lights in the expanse of the sky to separate the day from the night...'" (1:14 NIV).

According to the classic view, the sun, moon, and stars were created on the fourth day. On the fourth day God formed the heavenly bodies from the "unformed mass" of primeval material created on the first day.

Luther argued that the raw and unformed light created on the first day was brought to perfection on the fourth day by the addition of the sun, moon, and stars.[9] In the same way, Calvin argued that "in this verse Moses says nothing other than that God now purposed that certain sources should diffuse the [primeval] light throughout all the world."[10] Calvin then continued, "The [primeval] light was at first dispersed [without a source], but now it proceeded from physical light sources."[11]

4. The six days of creation refer to twenty-four-hour days.

Two distinct tendencies can be found in the classic view regarding the days of Genesis 1. Some stressed the all-powerful, sovereign work of God in creation. God did not need six days to create the world; He could have created it in a moment of time. Augustine said, "He who dwells in eternity created all things in a single instance."[12] Others pointed to God's accommodation to man's six-day work week as a way of becoming a part of his world.

Though the first group tended to minimize the importance of the six-day week of creation, both groups accepted the framework of creation given in Genesis 1. Both groups stressed that these six days were twenty-four hours in length. The idea that the six days of Genesis 1 were anything but twenty-four-hour days didn't spread widely until the need was felt to fit the creation account into the larger time periods demanded by astronomy and geography.[13]

With the development of the science of geology, the idea that the earth as we know it today could have been created in a single week of twenty-four-hour days was increasingly difficult to maintain. Geologists spoke of vastly long periods during which the earth was formed.

In the face of such theories, the classic view held fast to the notion of twenty-four-hour days, which it took to be the biblical meaning. There thus arose a need to reconcile those twenty-four-hour days with the lengthy geological ages. The early classic response to the long time periods of geological history took two, quite different, lines of defense.

1. The "flood geologists" argued that the geological record, which suggested an extended and lengthy period for the formation of the earth, was actually the result of the flood, not of creation itself.

2. The "restitutionists" — as those who held to the idea of the "gap theory" were called — argued that the period of six, twenty-four-hour days in Genesis 1 was not the time when God originally *created* the earth, but the time when God *restored* the earth after a great cataclysm.

A third group made a major modification to the classical view. They were the "concordists" who maintained that the long geological ages in the earth's history were to be identified with the six days of Genesis 1, each day representing an entire geological age. This position later became known as the "day-age" theory. The view was first developed by anti-deist theologians[14] and later by geologists and paleontologists.[15] The deists had maintained that God was not involved in the details of creation. Having created the world, God left it to itself; the world merely ran by itself, as a watch that has been wound up and left.

For the strongly pastoral Johann Friedrich Wilhelm Jerusalem (d. 1789), such a view was contradicted by the Genesis creation account. Genesis 1 was not an account of an early, six-day creation, after which God left the world to run its own course. Rather, Genesis 1 recounted God's ongoing involvement with the world over vast periods of geological history. Jerusalem maintained that what modern science knows about the age of the earth and the long geological ages during which the earth reached its present shape was already known to the biblical author. In the Genesis creation account, the author attempted to present his essentially modern scientific viewpoint in terms which his ancient and primitive readers would understand — a six-day week of twenty-four-hour days. When we read Genesis 1 today, Jerusalem argued, we must look beyond the literal imagery of the account to the scientific facts which the biblical author wished to convey.[16]

Jerusalem's view of the ancient biblical author suffered from the same kind of anachronistic thinking that plagued H. G. Wells in our own century. Wells envisioned a final war which would bring the end of the world, but the war he imagined necessarily took the form he was familiar with — conventional warfare with infantry, tanks, and airplanes. His final war thus dragged on for decades. Had he known of nuclear weapons developed at the end of the twentieth century, his last battle could have been reduced to a few hours or even minutes. Wells, like Jerusalem's author of Genesis, spoke of colossal events in conventional, contemporary terms.

5. *The scope of God's work over the six-day period is the "earth," along with the rest of the universe.*

It was always understood within the classic view that the scope of the creation account was universal; it was about the creation of the entire universe. The words "earth" and "heavens" in Genesis 1:1 were understood in their broadest sense. Yet there were two important qualifications of the term "earth" that, over the long run, rendered the meaning of Genesis 1 somewhat ambiguous.

First, the term "earth" in Genesis 1 was never understood in a strictly geophysical sense. The Hebrew term was never interpreted as referring to the totality of the "physical earth" which included the "seas" and the regions "under the earth." Instead, the "earth" was the region of dry land surrounded by the "seas." The term "earth" referred only to the uppermost level of dry ground. Anything below the surface of the "earth" was known as the region "under the earth."

Early maps of the earth show clearly how the term was understood. It referred to the place where animals and human beings dwelled, including both the habitable regions and the wilderness. It did not include the "skies" (where the birds fly) or the "seas" (where the fish swim). To speak of the classic view as referring to the whole earth, then, is a misnomer. It was the "whole earth" in a narrowly qualified sense.

Second, the scope of the term "earth" was further qualified as Western explorers ventured further and further from their homelands. Before the exploration of the New World, the meaning of the biblical term "earth" was confined to the known world. Throughout the Middle Ages, as Western society's understanding of the geographical extent of the earth began to expand, so did the meaning of the Hebrew term "earth" in Genesis 1.

The basic meaning of the term, of course, did not change; it continued to mean the whole surface of dry land, surrounded by the seas. Yet just as the scope of the Hebrew term "heavens" in Genesis 1 expanded with the invention of the telescope and the discovery of gravity, so also the scope of the term "earth" grew with the expanding knowledge of other worlds and of the civilizations which inhabited them. The term "earth" came to include all those regions beyond the horizon of Europe and the Middle East.

Our modern understanding of the term "earth" is both the same as and quite different from earlier ages. It is the same because both modern and ancient readers understood Genesis 1 to refer to the whole of the dry ground on the surface of the earth — the "land" surrounded by the sea. Yet the modern understanding differs from the ancient one in that it has been greatly expanded by the knowledge gained from exploration and travel. We have a much greater appreciation and understanding of the surface of the "earth" today than did ancient readers of Scripture.

Interestingly enough, modern Hebrew spoken in Israel today has preserved the earlier, more localized, meaning of "earth." It has done so, in effect, by coining another word for "world" or "earth" in a global sense. When it speaks of the "land" of Israel, for example, it uses the biblical term from Genesis 1. It does not use that term to refer to the "world at large."

Another interesting feature of the modern Hebrew meaning of the word "earth" is that, in its term for the "United States of America," modern Hebrew uses the plural form of the biblical word from Genesis 1. It means, literally, the "United Lands of America," or, the "United Earths of America." Thus in modern Hebrew the term "earth" in Genesis 1 is equivalent to the term "States" in the name "United States of America." Modern Hebrew has not allowed modern conceptions of "the world" to change the meaning of the biblical term. It has, rather, coined new Hebrew words to supply a broader range of meaning to the modern notions of "the world at large."

While both the older classic view and its modern equivalents may stress the comprehensive meaning of the term "earth" in Genesis 1:2, the exact scope of the term can vary greatly. Ultimately, we must seek the meaning of the term "earth" from the biblical text itself. Fortunately, there are clear clues within the text as to the extent of the Hebrew term for "earth" (see chapter 4).

GETTING CLOSER TO THE TRUTH

The classic view of Genesis 1 and 2, though often expressed in subtle ways through translations and unstated assumptions, represents a definite and distinct stream of interpretation. Its impact on our own understanding of the biblical creation account should not be overlooked. To do so would mean turning a blind eye to one of the most cogent forces at work in our interpretation of the text.

Much of real value can be found in the classic view. In fact, I believe subtle variations within this view contain genuine aspects of the original author's intent. For that reason, we must take a closer look at a few of those important variations within the classic view.

• Some scholars who held to the "classic view" of the
Genesis creation account also saw the scope of "the land"
described in Genesis 1:2–31 in limited terms. They understood it primarily to refer to "the land" later promised to
Abraham.

• Some scholars have held that the creation account in
Genesis 1 focuses primarily on God's preparation of the
garden of Eden.

CHAPTER TWENTY-THREE

THE CLASSIC VIEW, REVISED

Two important variations within the classic view of Genesis 1 and 2 deserve special mention and greatly affect our understanding of the creation account. Those two variations center on the precise meaning of the term "earth" in Genesis 1:2, and the precise location of the garden of Eden.

THE MEANING OF "EARTH" IN 1:2

Early interpreters of Genesis 1 were less than unanimous about the relationship between the term "earth" in the expression "heavens and earth" in Genesis 1:1 and the word "earth" when used alone in 1:2. Are these two verses speaking of the same "earth"? If so, what "earth" does the writer of Genesis have in mind?

The consensus among Christian scholars was that the word "earth" both in 1:1 and 1:2 referred to the whole of the inhabitable earth. In 1:1, the expression "heaven and earth" appears to divide the world into two distinct spheres: "heaven," the habitation of the angels; and "earth," the habitation of human beings.

According to the classic view, however, in 1:1 these two spheres had not yet been formed out of the primeval mass. "Heaven" and "earth" were still mixed in the huge, unformed chaos. Thus in the classic view there was little reason to discuss the precise meaning of "earth" in 1:1. The underlying assumption was that "earth" in 1:1 referred to the same unformed mass as in 1:2.

The meaning of the term in 1:2 was another question. Although Christian scholars fundamentally agreed, still much effort went into clarifying the exact scope and extent of this "earth." Christian scholarship remained largely under the influence of the Greek translation of Genesis, and in the end, two features of the Greek translation of 1:2 proved crucial.

1. The Septuagint had used the Greek term for "earth" to translate the Hebrew term "land" in verse 1:2. Thus the verse came to be understood as a description of the whole domain of human habitation. Almost from the start, Christian scholarship viewed 1:2 in cosmic, global terms.[1]

2. The Septuagint clearly read the phrase "formless and void" (*tohu wabohu*) in light of the Greek concept of primeval chaos. The "earth" in 1:2 was an unformed mass of material waiting to be formed into the world as we now know it. Hence the notion of the primeval earth as "formless and void" was deeply rooted in the Christian psyche.

JEWISH DISSENT

Some scholars viewed Genesis 1:2 from a quite different perspective. Medieval Jewish interpreters who had not been greatly influenced by the Septuagint understood the Hebrew term for "earth" in 1:2 in the more limited sense of the "promised land." In doing so they drew from an interpretive tradition grounded in the Hebrew text itself.

These scholars took the Hebrew term for "earth" to mean the land promised to the descendants of Abraham. It was perfectly natural for such biblical scholars to read their Hebrew text in this way; in Hebrew this was the very word used in those texts. Moreover, these men were well aware that God's promise of "the land" was a central theme in Genesis and the Pentateuch.

"The land" promised to Abraham and the patriarchs was quite large in biblical terms. It extended from the River Euphrates to the River of Egypt. That includes most of what we know today as the inhabited areas of the ancient Near East. It also corresponded to a large degree to what most medieval biblical scholars saw as the inhabited world (the "new worlds" later discovered by European explorers were not yet a part of their geographical perspective). Furthermore, the rivers which identified the promised land in Genesis 15 were precisely those which encompassed the garden of Eden in Genesis 2. It was natural, therefore, for these scholars to understand that the creation account centered on the promised land. They drew their maps from the descriptions of "the land" which they found in Scripture. Their view of the extent of the "earth" was drawn from these texts, not the other way around.

The medieval Jewish commentator Rashi understood most of the account of Genesis 1 as a direct reference to God's preparation of the promised land. Rashi gave much thought to the reason Genesis, and the Pentateuch as a whole, would begin with an account of the creation of the promised land. As usual, his answer was insightful and betrayed a vast appreciation for the purpose of Scripture.

Rashi argued that God began with an account of the creation of the promised land because He wanted to show Israel and the nations that "the land" was His and He could give it to whomever He pleased. Moses thus had a clear ethical and theological motive in mind as he began writing the Pentateuch. Should the peoples of the world accuse Israel of stealing the land from the Canaanites, Israel need only reply that "the land" belonged to God. Rashi said, "God created the land and he will give it to whomever he pleases. In his good pleasure he gave it to the Canaanites, and in his good pleasure he took it from them and gave it to us."[2] The issue of who had the most legitimate claim to the promised land was crucial in Rashi's own day; he lived during the time of the first crusades in the eleventh century.

Both the thought and the Hebrew phraseology of Rashi's comments were taken directly from the Book of Jeremiah. In Jeremiah 27, the prophet was called by God to proclaim to Israel and the Canaanite nations that the Lord was about to deliver them as captives into the hands of the Babylonians. Through Jeremiah, God said, "With my great power and outstretched arm I made the land, human beings, and the animals which are upon the land, and I will give it to whomever I please. The time has come when I will put all these lands into the hand of Nebuchadnezzar, the king of Babylon" (Jeremiah 27:5–6).

It was obvious to early Jewish interpreters that the word "land" in the Jeremiah passage meant "the land" which was promised to Israel and which was also inhabited by Edom, Moab, Ammon, Tyre, and Sidon (Jeremiah 27:3). It was also clear to them, as it is to most modern scholars, that the Jeremiah passage was reading off the pages of Genesis 1. It was natural for these early Jewish commentators to interpret Genesis 1 along the same lines as it had been read by the prophet Jeremiah. Thus they assumed the creation account described God's creation of the promised land.

These medieval Jewish commentators were followed by some noted Christian scholars. According to John Lightfoote — a widely read biblical exegete, theologian, and a Christian scholar of considerable standing — the Genesis account of creation describes God's preparation of a specific area of land which he identified as the garden of Eden.[3] Lightfoote held that 1:1 states that God created the universe, but from 1:2 through the end of the chapter, the passage focuses on God's preparation of the land that was to be the garden of Eden. Lightfoote's view was developed further by later Christian scholars.[4]

LOCATION OF THE GARDEN OF EDEN

Before the sixteenth century, Christian and Jewish views of the garden of Eden were based largely on a spiritual or allegorical interpretation of the Bible. For Christians, the "paradise" described in Genesis 2 was identified with the "paradise" which Jesus spoke of in John 14 — a paradise in heaven. Thus the garden of Eden became part heavenly and part earthly, an abode linking heaven with earth. Its location was understood vaguely to be somewhere in a far-off place.[5] Such views of Eden were shaped by two important facts.

1. There was very little knowledge of the larger world among Bible students of that day.

2. Classical mythologies played a key role in shaping the world views of early Christianity.[6]

The sixteenth century marked a major turning point in the identification of the garden of Eden — one that mixed biblical realism with geographical data. The key transitional stage was a work by Badian von St. Gallen called *Trium terrae partium Epitome* (1534/48). Badian taught that the whole world was the paradise of Genesis 2 and that before the Fall, the world was a place of great joy and desire. After the Fall, however, the world was reduced to a place of great misery. The one river which flowed out of the garden in Genesis 2 was the ocean. The four rivers that branched off from it were the Ganges, Nile, Tigris, and Euphrates. Along with the ocean, these rivers, according to Badian, divided the world into West, South, East, and North.

Luther was the first to reject Badian's view in his commentary on Genesis (*Enarrationes in Genesin*, 1524). The major problem of Badian's commentary, Luther thought, was that it did not fit the geographical features of the area. Moreover, Badian's view did not square with the biblical account in which Adam and Eve were cast out of the garden eastward; neither did it fit with the biblical notion of the neighboring countries of Cush, Havilah, and Assur. Finally, Luther argued, it did not make sense to identify a river with the ocean.

Luther thus broke fundamentally with the earlier views of paradise. He distinguished between the paradise in Genesis 2 and that of the New Testament, and he rejected the allegorical interpretation of paradise. Luther maintained that the original location of the garden of Eden, though known to Adam and his descendants, was obliterated by the devastating effects of Noah's flood. The geographical conditions of that region had changed significantly, including the rivers which served as the borders of the garden.[7]

Luther's view carried the field throughout the whole of the period of Orthodoxy and beyond. It closed the door to outright identification of the garden with existing geography but also left the door open to seeking clues to its location among the remains of the flood. After Luther, there was growing interest in identifying the exact location of the garden through contemporary geographical study. Luther's underlying assumption was that the four rivers originated in the garden, each flowing out of one river.

<h2 style="text-align:center">EFFORTS TO LOCATE THE GARDEN</h2>

In the late seventeenth century, David Clericus[8] said certain clues suggested the garden had been located in Syria. Syria was described by the prophets as a paradise and early geographers (Strabo, Plinius, Ptolomaeus) knew of a city near the source of the Orontes River named Paradeisos. Moreover, there were four rivers in that region whose names Clericus was confident he could relate to the four rivers of Genesis 2.[9]

In the early eighteenth century, Jean Hardouin[10] believed he had found clues which pointed to Palestine as the location of the garden of Eden. Based on various arguments, Hadrian Reland[11] located the garden in upper Armenia. He put forward three primary arguments:

1. Armenia was the source of the Tigris and Euphrates rivers.

2. The rivers Pishon and Gihon must share the same source as the Tigris and Euphrates; therefore they must be the Phasis and Araxes rivers in the region of Armenia.

3. The idea of a single river from which the four rivers of Eden flowed resulted from viewing the rivers in light of a single geographical area, namely Armenia. The original river might have disappeared or become an underground river after the flood.

Each of these attempts followed Martin Luther's break with the medieval idea that the garden of Eden was located in a semi-heavenly abode. They all attempted to find the remains of the physical location of the garden after it was destroyed by the flood. The key had generally been the location of the two well-known rivers, the Tigris and the Euphrates. In most cases the location of the garden was taken to be near, or identical with, the promised land. There were, of course, a few exceptions. The seventeenth century Swedish scholar, Olaus Rudbeck of Upsala, published a scholarly work defending his own unlikely (but understandable) thesis that the garden of Eden had been located in Sweden.

TEXTUAL CLUES TO THE GARDEN'S LOCATION

John Calvin suggested a new view of the location of the garden of Eden, based on two important textual observations. First, Calvin noted that the garden was situated "on the East," which he took to mean east of the land of Judah.[12] Second, Calvin noted that according to the Genesis text, only one river flowed through the garden itself. From there the river parted into "four heads." Those "heads," argued Calvin, were to be found on either side of the garden — two heads leading into the garden and thus joined in the one river that passed through it. The other two heads were formed as the river flowed out of the garden and forked off into two rivers. Thus on either side of the garden, the river that passed through the garden forked off into two rivers. On one side of the garden, the Tigris and Euphrates flowed into it. On the other side, the Pishon and the Gihon flowed out of it.

Calvin then amassed arguments from ancient geographers to show that the Tigris and Euphrates flowed together for some distance before splitting off again. It was at that spot that Calvin located the garden. Many Christian biblical scholars followed Calvin's interpretation. Its great value was that it took its clues from the narrative text, rather than from contemporary geography.

Thus there have been two primary methods of identifying the location of the garden of Eden. The approach taken by Luther assumed that the exact site could not be identified because the garden had been destroyed by Noah's flood. Despite that, however, Luther and others did attempt to find evidence of its location. The approach taken by Calvin attempted to interpret the textual data in such a way that a contemporary site could be identified.

To the extent that modern biblical commentaries understand Genesis 2 in realistic and literal terms, the approach of Calvin is still followed. Like Calvin, most modern attempts at identifying the garden of Eden center on Mesopotamia.

There is room for a new look at the location of the garden of Eden in Genesis 2 — one that is primarily textual in its orientation. Like Calvin, it seeks to understand how the biblical author described its location; but unlike Calvin, it doesn't interpret the textual data in light of extrabiblical clues.

Where then, within the world of the text of Genesis itself, is the garden of Eden? And why are the same rivers cited as the boundaries for the garden of Eden and for the promised land? Does the author of the Pentateuch wish his readers to consider these two key locations as identical? In *Genesis Unbound*, that is exactly what I have contended. I have argued that for the writer of the Pentateuch, the garden of Eden was located in the promised land.

This is not an entirely new view. Several Christian scholars have located the garden of Eden somewhere within the boundaries of the biblical "promised land." In the seventeenth century, for example, the Reformed biblical scholar Johann Heidegger located the garden in a valley near the city of Jericho. A common view among early rabbis was that Adam was created from the same ground where the temple was later built, that is, in Jerusalem.

The location of the garden of Eden is important if we are to properly interpret Genesis 1 and 2 because of the close relationship between the events described in those two chapters. In the present shape of the text, the author clearly intends us to identify the events in Genesis 2 as a sort of close-up view of the events of Genesis 1. If the garden of Eden in Genesis 2 is identified as the land later promised to Abraham and his seed, then it is likely that the author also wants us to read the account in Genesis 1 within that same context. The question of the location of the garden of Eden greatly effects the larger question of the scope of the creation account in Genesis 1:2–2:4a.

It also affects our understanding of God's overall plans and purposes in the Bible. In the Pentateuch we see that, in the covenant at Sinai and the promises to Abraham, God offered Israel the opportunity to return to the "good land" He had prepared for them. It was a blessed land (Deuteronomy 28:2–12). He intended it for their nourishment and enjoyment. They could dwell there as long as they obeyed Him and kept His commandments. Even though in their disobedience they may lose their land, God promised to return them to it when He established His New Covenant with their descendants (Deuteronomy 30:1–11). Israel's hope for God's future blessing is thus embodied in the picture of divine blessing in the land that is described in these early chapters of Genesis.

TO THE LAW AND TO THE TESTIMONY!

Many other important issues are related to a thorough understanding of the biblical account of creation. I have attempted to isolate and give adequate treatment to some I believe are crucial.

Central to my understanding of the early chapters of Genesis is the attempt to read these chapters within the larger context of the other narratives in the Book of Genesis and the Pentateuch. I believe modern readers of these chapters have grown accustomed to certain basic assumptions about Genesis 1 and 2. Those assumptions may, in the end, prove to be correct. They may also prove to be inadequate and lead to a fundamental misreading of the author's intent in these chapters.

In the end, we would all do well to go back and read the text again. Nothing can take the place of an open, careful scrutiny of the text itself. Our interpretations will wear thin and ultimately pass away with time. But the biblical text, and it alone, thank God, will remain for future generations to continue to read and ponder.

Later interpreters may look at our efforts and find that they cast some measure of light on God's Word. Others may think these efforts have entirely missed the mark. What they must do, however, is the same thing we ourselves must do in our own day. We must let the text speak for itself and let it decide the matter.

All of our views on this important topic ultimately fall under the same judgment as the opinions of the so-called authorities in the days of the prophet Isaiah. When confronted with the views of the scholars of his day, the prophet advised, "Go to the Law and the Testimonies" — that is, "Go to the Scriptures themselves." And if the views of the scholars don't conform to the words of Scripture themselves, "then there is no light at all in their opinions" (Isaiah 8:20).

And there the matter must rest.

THERE YOU HAVE IT

Just this morning a pastor stopped by my office to tell me of the struggles he was having with his congregation over Genesis 1. His complaint was a common one. "Why can't folks just read Genesis 1 for what it says?" he lamented. "Why do they always have to ask how it relates to science?"

Although I'm sympathetic to his concern, I think there *is* a place for asking how the early chapters of the Bible relate to science. After all, the Bible does seem to imply that it is describing actual events. It does seem to suggest that we are to read it literally. If Genesis 1 were written as poetry, we might have grounds for saying it should not be read literally or realistically — but it's not poetry. It's written as a straightforward account of God's work and thus invites us to read it literally and realistically.

But where does that put us with modern science? Must we tell our children when we send them off to school that the universe was created in six days and that the sun, moon, and stars were not formed until the fourth day? Must we tell them that this all happened just a few thousand years ago? Must we tell them that Noah's ark was stuffed with every kind of dinosaur, pterosaur, and ancient mammal that ever existed? Certainly we must, if that's what the Bible actually teaches. But the question I have tried to raise in this book is, does the Bible really teach such a thing? Since you've reached the epilogue, I assume you know that I don't believe it does.

What I have attempted to show in *Genesis Unbound* is that the biblical account of creation in Genesis 1 and 2, when left to itself, gives us a highly plausible account of God's work of creation. God created the universe "in the beginning." How long ago was that? We don't know. What we know from Genesis 1:1 is that the world we see around us today came into being through an act of God. It did not exist in eternity past; God created it. We also know that God created the universe during an indeterminate period covered by the "beginning" in verse 1, not during the six days described in the rest of Genesis 1. That time may have been millions, or even billions, of years — the text simply doesn't say.

What, then, did God do during the six-day week recorded in the rest of the chapter? As I see it, the author of Genesis and the Pentateuch sees God's work during that week focused primarily on the "promised land." He wants his readers to see that the same land God later promised to Abraham (Genesis 15) and then gave to Israel (Exodus 19) had already been prepared for Adam and Eve at the beginning of recorded history. They could enjoy that land as long as they were obedient. If they were not obedient, they were to be cast out of the land in exile. The fate of Adam and Eve foreshadowed that of Israel in later history. The Israelites proved to be disobedient and thus faced the consequences of God's judgment.

I am well aware that not everyone will like, let alone accept, the basic thesis I have presented here. My purpose has not been to convince everyone. Rather, I have tried to provide an understanding of the first chapters of Genesis that is both literal and faithful to the intention of the author of the Pentateuch.

I think it is unfortunate that when a person supports a literal interpretation of Genesis 1, he or she is given only one choice. In our day the word "creationism" has come to mean only one thing, the belief that God created the universe in a single, six-day week. That, unfortunately, has been the only game in town. I have tried to show that another view can equally well be called "creationism." It, too, believes the Bible speaks about a literal six-day week, but it sees that week as describing the preparation of the promised land, not the creation of the universe. To be sure, Genesis 1:1

does indeed teach that God created the whole universe, but the rest of the chapter (1:2–31) is about His preparing the promised land.

Whether you consider my interpretation as valid depends on your further study of this text. Don't take my word for it! Read the text and attempt to understand it within the context of both the Book of Genesis and the rest of the Pentateuch. I believe I have come close to capturing the original author's sense of the text. I'm satisfied that I have at least given readers an alternative for viewing this important part of Scripture — an alternative that I believe is faithful to the text, that takes it in a literal and realistic way, and that doesn't ask it to do handstands in order to conform to modern scientific theory.

Now may the Lord be pleased to use it in whatever way gives Him the most glory.

LITERAL, FIGURATIVE, OR SOMETHING ELSE?

In this appendix I want to turn our attention to the basic interpretive issues behind most modern attempts to understand Genesis 1 and 2. The central issue is, Was the Genesis creation account intended to be understood literally or figuratively?

Most readers of Genesis 1 and 2 would probably agree that when read at face value, the creation account in Genesis 1 is a straightforward description of God's work. It describes the events of creation in simple, historical terms. It tells us what God did and is written in simple historical narrative.

Although many have interpreted the creation account as if it were poetic, there are no signs that these texts were intended to be read as such. To be sure, the texts are written in a structured, balanced, narrative style, and repetition is frequently used. But in themselves, such features do not indicate the presence of poetry.

POETRY VS. NARRATIVE

Poetry as it is known in the rest of the Bible has distinct features which simply are not found in the narratives of Genesis 1 and 2. Compare the narrative account of creation in Genesis 1 with the poetic version of creation in Job 38. The key clue that Job 38 is poetry is the "parallelism" of its lines. Biblical poetry is structured around a basic pattern of repetition called parallelism. An idea is stated once, and then it is immediately restated, or contrasted, by a second statement. Two such lines of poetry are said to be "parallel."

Another clue that Job 38 is poetry, and not narrative, is the presence of meter. Meter simply denotes that poetic lines in parallelism are balanced. They are approximately the same length, whether that length is measured in words per line or syllables. Poetry also is marked by highly figurative language. Each line of biblical poetry is characterized by a distinct "figure" or poetic image.

There are always two questions to ask of biblical poetry. The first is, What is its meaning? The second is, What is it about? To ask about the *meaning* of a poem is to ask what image it contains and how it develops that image. What does that image intend to say to the reader? What response does the image attempt to evoke from the reader? To ask what a poem is *about* is to investigate its subject. Is it about God and creation? Is it about Israel and God's covenants? There are many "subjects" which biblical poetry addresses.

Unlike biblical poetry, biblical narrative is highly realistic. It describes persons and events "just as they happened." Narratives tell us in a realistic way what they are about. Genesis 1 and 2, for example, are clearly about creation. Those chapters have the same subject matter as Job 38, but they are narrative.

Job 38 is a poetic text. In clearly poetic lines, God's work of creation is compared to building a house. God says to Job, "Where were you when I laid the earth's foundation?... Who marked off its dimensions?... Who stretched a measuring line across it? On what were its footings set or who laid its cornerstone?" (Job 38:4–6).

The imagery of this poetry is not hard to see. The poem simply describes God as a builder. He makes a house. The subject matter which the imagery points to can be seen in the first line, which refers to the "earth's foundation." What is being described? God's "building" the earth.

In the same passage, creation is also compared to the birth of a baby: "Who shut up the sea behind doors when it burst forth from the womb, when I made the clouds its diapers (NIV, "garment") and wrapped it in swaddling bands (NIV, "thick darkness")...?" (Job 38:8–9). As is frequently the case, English translators have blurred the imagery; nevertheless, one can see from these examples that poetry uses figures of speech. It compares actual events with picturesque images from everyday life. Narrative, on the other hand, gives a realistic account of actual events. That is what we find in Genesis 1 and 2.

MYTH

For most of its history, the creation account in Genesis 1 and 2 was understood as a literal depiction of God's work in the past. To explain the meaning of the text was considered the best way to understand the origin of the world. The creation account was understood as a literal description of the first stages of the history of the world and of the human race. It defined the Western world's understanding of reality.

In the modern era, which began in earnest as far back as the eighteenth century, the biblical account of creation began to lose its absolute claim on reality. The realism of its narrative depiction was increasingly overlooked. Eventually, its version of creation was supplanted by scientific ones. No longer could its straightforward prose be understood literally and realistically. To be sure, many conservative and orthodox interpreters of Genesis 1 continued to read Genesis literally and factually. They, however, were increasingly marginalized as spokesmen for the meaning of the text.

Others, however, maintained that these narratives were never meant to be read literally and realistically. These texts, they say, never described real events. They were always and only mere stories, symbols, or myths of a bygone era. They represented one of the ways ancient societies explained their world. Their purpose was not to explain how the world was created but to say that the world is a place where human beings can feel at home with God.

In this view, Genesis 1 and 2 tell us that human beings belong in this world. They have a purpose, which can be discovered through the narrative stories that follow the creation account. These stories put a face on the universal feeling of dependence which human beings sense. As such, these stories are not to be understood as "historical" and should not be interpreted literally. They are myths.

A "myth" in modern parlance is an explanation of reality. Myths are not actual depictions of the world but are stories which attempt to reveal basic truths that lie behind the events of this world.

In recent years, it has generally been recognized that there are serious problems with "mythological" interpretations of the biblical creation account. To be sure, myths did exist in the ancient world. Many primitive cultures still rely heavily on myths to explain their basic understanding of the world. Myths give societies their sense of identity.

The use of "myth" to explain the biblical creation narratives, however, has run into serious trouble. For one thing, the biblical texts do not look like myths. Ancient myths were, as far as we know, always poetic. Poetry was a defining characteristic of ancient mythology.

As we have them in Genesis 1, the biblical stories of creation are anything but poetry; they are historical narrative. The fact that they are written in narrative form rather than poetry shows that at least their author understood them as real accounts of God's work in creation.

Judging from what we know about ancient creation myths, the biblical texts give every impression of having been written and understood as realistic depictions of actual events. It simply will not do to say that the Genesis creation accounts are merely ancient myths and thus should not be taken literally. If we are to respect the form in which we now have them — as narrative — we must reckon with the fact that they are intended to be read as literal accounts of God's activity in creation.

What has just been said about Genesis 1 and "myth" is now widely acknowledged by biblical scholars. Yet some have attempted to retain the notion of "myth" in Genesis 1 by looking behind the biblical texts as we now have them. They acknowledge that the text as it stands in the Bible today is not myth. But they conjecture that the biblical stories of creation originally may not have been narrative. Couldn't the biblical story of creation have been circulated at an earlier time in poetic form? At that stage, then, it would have been understood as myth.

The problem with such an approach is that it is almost entirely conjectural. We have no copies of Genesis 1 in poetic form. Nor are there compelling reasons to believe the text of Genesis was originally poetic. Years ago biblical scholars believed they could detect signs of poetic meter within the Genesis narratives, but few would argue that today. It is extremely difficult and risky business to discuss the form of a text about which we know nothing and of which we have no examples.

The narrative of Genesis 1 as we have it today is just that, a narrative. If it was poetry at an earlier stage, there is no evidence for it. Genesis 1 and 2 are today acknowledged to be historical narrative and not poetry. The idea that these narratives are myth, therefore, is nearly impossible to maintain. As we now have them, Genesis 1 and 2 have all the appearances of a literal, historical account of creation. Consequently, our concern should be to explain the intent of the narrative of Genesis 1 as we now have it in the Bible.

MYTH, REVISED

Sometimes the word "myth" is used in a quite different sense. "Myth," as sociologists and anthropologists sometimes understand it, is merely a cultural mechanism by which groups of people identify themselves. As such, myths can take many forms. They can be poetic, but they may also be stories and historical accounts. Myths tell people who they are. People and nations identify themselves by telling stories of their past and of the founding of their countries. When used in that sense, the term "myth" does not necessarily imply that the stories are untrue. In fact, those who told the stories often expected them to be understood as true.

Many today understand Genesis 1 and 2 to be "myths" in this broader sense. Critical biblical scholars who would not for a minute say the biblical narratives were accurate accounts of the past would, nevertheless, say that their author intended them to be taken as actual history. The biblical authors, they say, intended to write about the actual creation of the world, but being naive ancient storytellers, they simply got their facts wrong.

Hermann Gunkel, a leading biblical critic in the early part of this century, believed the author of Genesis 1 was very much of a "scientist" by intent. He wanted to record the actual process of the formation of the world. The only problem, Gunkel maintained, was that he got his facts wrong. He relied on faulty documents and stories that were simply naive and inaccurate. Gunkel's description of the purpose behind the creation narrative in Genesis 1 gives a helpful insight into his understanding of the historical interest of the author of the final version of the Pentateuch: "He was not a poet who attempted to comprehend the material in a living way and to describe it visually, but rather he was a scientific person who desired to penetrate to the very nature of the thing itself and who wanted to divide the whole of the data into classes and reflect on the various characteristics of the classes. Even though these classes may appear to us quite simple, nevertheless they reflect the work of a real scientific spirit."[1]

Suppose a second grade history teacher tells her class that George Washington crossed the Delaware River and surprised the British. Such a story is intended both to give historical information about the Revolutionary War and to inspire courage and resourcefulness in the students. The story gives identity to the students when they see the story of George Washington as their story as well. When they hear the story, the students become part of a rich heritage and cultural fabric that honors those basic virtues. When the story is told, the students are naturally led to believe that George Washington actually crossed the Delaware River and that there really was a Revolutionary War. It's a true story — that, at least, is how it's intended.

Nevertheless, some modern scholars would call that story a "myth" — not because it is an inaccurate account of what happened to George

Washington, but because the story plays an important role in providing a basic identity for the students. It helps them understand who they are and what they stand for.

The term "myth" is thus an ambiguous word. For that reason it is not an appropriate description of the literary characteristics of Genesis 1, nor is it a clear and distinct way to describe the overall purpose of the creation account. It is unfortunate that the term "myth" is still used to describe Genesis 1.

POETRY-LIKE?

What should we call the type of narrative we find in Genesis 1 and 2? Many evangelical interpreters search for a more adequate way to describe the literary and historical intent of the creation account. An increasing number of evangelicals are reluctant to read those narratives as purely historical accounts. If read as literal history, they believe, the creation narrative would radically conflict with our modern scientific view of the origin of the world.

They are convinced that Genesis 1 teaches the earth and the universe are only a few thousand years old. They believe Genesis 1 teaches that the whole universe was created in six days and that the sun, moon, and stars were formed on the fourth day — two days before human beings were created. If that were the meaning of Genesis 1, it would fundamentally conflict with our modern understanding of the world.

In response, therefore, one often hears evangelicals describe the nature of these early Genesis narratives as "poetry-like." If these narratives are "poetry-like," we might be able to read them less literally. We might be able to look for truth in them apart from what they appear to be saying about the days of creation and the age of the universe.

There are serious problems, however, with the notion that Genesis 1 is "poetry-like." The idea hasn't received wide acceptance among Old Testament scholars because there simply is little in the text to support reading it "like" poetry. It is clearly narrative. So while some evangelicals may continue to describe Genesis 1 as "poetry-like," biblical scholars generally are not convinced. On the face of it, such a notion appears to dismiss the obvious intent of these narratives to tell us, in literal terms, what actually happened at creation.

Let's consider this question from another perspective. Have you heard any debates about the relationship between "science and the Bible" when it comes to the poetic descriptions of creation in Job 38? No one gets upset when God is pictured as a carpenter, making a house. Why have debates raged around Genesis 1, but not Job 38? The answer is obvious. Job 38 is transparently poetic, and we naturally accept its images as nonliteral depictions of reality. Genesis 1, however, is clearly different from Job 38. Genesis 1 has no signs of poetry. It is definitely narrative and hence a quite different kind of literature than poetry. When we read narratives, we believe they depict reality for us in literal and realistic terms. That is what the rest of the biblical narratives do, and hence the same expectations arise in us as we read Genesis 1.

Surely the narratives of Genesis 1 and 2 are highly stylized and show many signs of being shaped and artfully composed. That, however, does not make them poetry. It also does not make them "poetry-like." Virtually all biblical narratives are shaped and artfully composed, but that doesn't make them poetry, or even "poetry-like." It may be convenient to dismiss the intent of the author of Genesis 1 and 2 as figurative, but it is extremely difficult to do so on the basis of what we find in the texts themselves. There is, in fact, a growing awareness of this among recent evangelical works on Genesis.

META-HISTORY?

Recent evangelical studies of Genesis 1 and 2 are characterized by another approach to these narratives. A growing number of evangelicals have come to accept that the early narratives in Genesis — though realistic and hence not poetry — nevertheless are not "history" in the strict sense of the term. Those narratives, they argue, are a kind of "supplementary-history" to the rest of Scripture. The creation account, they say, is an attempt to describe events that lie "above" or "beyond" the normal course of historical events. The biblical narratives are given a kind of supplemental preface to their history. In that preface events are described which are not to be understood as actual, historical events. The events are rather a history-like way of describing that God created the world and set nature and history in motion and hence continues to work though nature and history today.

The term often used to describe this kind of narrative is "meta-history." Literally, the expression "meta-history" means "with-history." The expression attempts to come to terms with what some take to be the dual nature of the Genesis narratives. They are both real history and, at the same time, supplemental to real history. They are history because they accurately describe real events. At the same time, however, they describe real events in a way that puts them beyond the normal processes of history writing. The Genesis narratives, they say, describe the real events of creation in a way that makes it look like ordinary history. Creation, however, was anything but an ordinary historical event.

Paradoxically, if the biblical notion of divine creation is true, they say, then the biblical account of creation cannot be understood literally and realistically. The biblical account presents creation as a historical event, but the point of the biblical account is that creation was an event that preceded history. The very concept of a "historical account" of creation, it is urged, demands a broader category such as "supplementary-history."

Acts of creation do not happen in our everyday experience of the world. Creation is a one-time event, an "unnatural" process. We do not see creation happening everyday. In fact, we never see new worlds being created around us "out of nothing." We may see an explosion in the heavens which will lead to the formation of a new star, but that is not "creation out of nothing." Even the notion of a "Big Bang" as the origin of our universe does not tell us anything about creation. The natural question that the "Big Bang" theory raises is, Where did the original mass of matter come from which exploded in the "Big Bang"? The "Big Bang" theory tries to explain only where our present universe came from; it does not explain where the original mass of material originated. If we saw a genuine act of creation in our world, we would have to call it a miracle. Such an event as a genuine "creation out of nothing," therefore, necessarily lies outside the range of our normal methods of historical investigation.

We must recognize, many say, that in reading Genesis 1 the narratives are attempting to write about a real event — namely, creation — but they necessarily cannot do so realistically or literally. The Genesis creation narrative is thus a story intended to portray a historical truth that lies beyond the actual story itself and its world. We must not, they say, confuse the world of the story with the real events which the story is attempting to portray.

It is important to recognize that the concept of a "supplementary-history" doesn't claim the stories of Genesis 1 are myths. As most evangelicals see them, these stories have real, historical events as their reference. But according to this view, the stories in Genesis 1 do not refer to those historical events literally. They represent them in realistic, rather than literal, terms.

The narratives in Genesis 1 and 2 tell us that an actual "creation out of nothing" occurred at the beginning of this world. They do so by portraying the work of God in realistic terms. God went about His work of making the world just as men or women go about their work on any given week. He then rested on the seventh day. God did not literally work six days and then literally rest on the seventh day; that is merely the way the author pictures God's work of creation. We do not have an account of creation that is both realistic and literal. We only have one that is realistic, but not literal.

According to this approach, then, Genesis 1 is a realistic story that is "added to" the earlier history of Israel. As a story it is not intended to be taken literally but to be understood as an expression or statement of a basic historical fact.

In that regard, the creation account is similar to the realistic story which Nathan the prophet told David in order to convict him of his sin with Bathsheba (2 Samuel 12:1–16). Nathan's story was about a real event, and it was told to David realistically. Nathan's story, however, casts that event in the form of a nonliteral story.[2] A real David took the wife of Uriah the Hittite. Nathan's story portrays that historical fact by recounting the realistic (but not literal) story of a wealthy landowner who steals a little sheep from a poor laborer, even though the wealthy man doesn't need it.

The concept that Genesis 1 and 2 is "meta-history" understands the creation account in much the same way. There actually was a divine creation; it was a historical fact. The account we have of it, however, is cast in a realistic but nonliteral narrative.

WEAKNESSES OF META-HISTORY

This is not, however, the view of the Genesis account represented in *Genesis Unbound*. The primary weakness of such a view of Genesis 1 is that it finds little support within the text itself. A straightforward reading of Genesis 1 and 2 gives every impression that the events happened just as they are described. It is intended to be read both realistically and literally. Genesis 1 *was* taken at face value as describing historical events by virtually all its readers for most of its history. Even those who rejected the plain meaning of the text in favor of finding a "spiritual truth" hidden in its words were quick to admit that its "plain meaning" was still intended to be understood as literal and historical.

Genesis 1 is presented as a story. That much is clear. But the story gives no clues that it is not also a true story, a literal depiction of what happened.

The story Nathan told David, on the other hand, has internal clues which alert the reader not to take it literally. The two men in the story are not identified as specific individuals, as they would be in an actual historical account (see 1 Samuel 1:1–3 for comparison); nor is the town where they lived identified. Nathan simply begins his story with a general description of the characters and the city, "There were two men in a certain town, one rich and the other poor..." (2 Samuel 12:1). Yet even with such "generic" features as clues, David understood the story as literal. At the conclusion of the story, David said to Nathan, "The man who has done this will surely be put to death" (2 Samuel 12:5). Nathan's answer to David, however, indicates that the author of the story (Nathan) understood the story in a nonliteral way. Nathan said to David, "You are the man!" (2 Samuel 12:7).

Compare this story with the narrative at the opening of 1 Samuel, which is rich in specific details about actual people and places, "There was a man from Ramathaim, a Zuphite from the hill country of Ephraim, whose name was Elkanah son of Jeroham, the son of Elihu, the son of Tohu, the son of Zuph, an Ephraimite." The presence of historical, specific features in the 1 Samuel 1 passage is an obvious clue that the story is to be understood literally. The lack of those same features in Nathan's story indicates it is to be understood nonliterally.[3]

In Genesis 1 and 2, the names of Adam and Eve are given, as well as the place where they lived. That suggests that the early narratives of the Pentateuch — in their final form, at least — were intended to be taken both realistically and literally.

Further support for understanding Genesis 1 and 2 as (at least) intending to be actual history is that the narrative form of Genesis 1 doesn't differ from the rest of the narrative texts in the Pentateuch and historical books. The patterns and narrative structures that are so evident in Genesis 1 are found with equal frequency in the narratives which deal with Israel's sojourn in Egypt and their wilderness wandering. They are, in fact, the same as those in the later biblical narratives dealing with the lives of David and Solomon and the kings of Israel and Judah.

If we take those narratives as realistic and literal — which most evangelicals do — then there is little basis for not doing so in Genesis 1. Both texts have miraculous events; hence both texts are not easily subject to the usual forms of historical investigation. The fact that we cannot easily investigate their historical worth doesn't indicate that they do not intend to record realistic and literal historical accounts. The historical problem lies in what they are attempting to describe, namely, miraculous events. The problem does not rest in their attempt to describe them.

Having said that, we can readily acknowledge that Genesis 1 is unique historical narrative. But it is unique by virtue of its subject matter, not by virtue of its form. It looks and acts like all other narrative.

The creation narratives in Genesis 1 and 2 are distinct from other biblical narratives because of their subject matter — creation — not because of their form — narrative. Therefore it may be helpful to devise a term which distinguishes the narrative in Genesis 1, on the basis of its subject matter, from most other biblical narratives.

Genesis 1 is a history about a unique event, creation. When we talk about history and historical events, however, we usually have in mind events that correspond to our own experiences. For us, the past is linked to the present and therefore shares certain basic features with our present world. The past is like the present. Historical events are similar to events in our own day. There is a real analogy between our world and the past.

In the historical events recorded in Genesis 1, however, we are taken into a world that is larger than, and greater than, our own everyday world. The narrative of Genesis 1 tells us things about our world which we would have no other means of knowing. It takes us beyond the boundaries of our historical and scientific knowledge. What is unique and important about Genesis 1 is that, from a literary standpoint, it does so literally and realistically. In its literal description of our world it does not stop at the boundaries of human understanding. It continues to describe literally and realistically aspects of our world known only to its Creator.

MEGA-HISTORY

One of the most natural questions people raise about Genesis 1 and 2 is how the author came to know about the events recorded in these chapters. Throughout most of the events in these chapters there were no human observers. Did God write these chapters? Did God dictate these chapters to Adam or to Moses? A common explanation in the past has been that God told Adam the story of creation when he was still in the garden of Eden. Adam then passed on the story, ultimately through Noah and then Abraham, and then on to Moses. There is, of course, no evidence of that in the text itself. The honest conclusion is that we simply do not know where the story of creation in Genesis 1 came from.

In looking for a distinct term to describe the kind of "historical" text we find in Genesis 1, I prefer to use the notion "mega-history." Literally the term "mega-history" means "huge-history." The biblical creation narratives are dealing with subject matter much "greater-than" the course of events in everyday historical experience. "History," in a technical sense, attempts to describe past events in categories that are true for everyday experience.

In that sense, as we saw in the discussion of "meta-history," a "history of creation" is difficult to imagine. How could we ever conceive of God's creating the universe in terms of our own historical experiences? Our own historical experiences would be impossible without creation. Without creation there would be no history at all. Thus creation comes at "the beginning" of history. It does not come within history but at its beginning. How, then, could creation ever be described as a simple historical event? Can we imagine a creation account which opens with the words, "In the first year of the reign of King Josiah, God created the heavens and the earth"? That is obviously impossible, absurd.

History is a result of creation. It cannot be the framework within which we understand creation. To understand creation we must have a larger framework than mere "history." We need a "mega-historical" framework. We need a history that includes but extends beyond the ranges of mere history.

In a way, writing a "history of creation" is like trying to write an autobiography that begins with a first-person account of one's own birth. By definition, an autobiography is a first-person account of one's life. Its perspective is therefore limited to the horizons of the author's own observations. That is what distinguishes an autobiography from a biography.

One could write a biography of one's own life, as well as an autobiography. The two are not the same. An autobiography is told within the limitations of one's own observations. For that reason few autobiographies begin with a first-person account of the author's birth. One's own birth is a real event and an essential part of one's life, but it does not fall within the range of the subject matter of an autobiography. An attempt to write such an autobiography would necessitate a kind of "mega-autobiography," one that is greater than the range of one's own everyday experiences of life.

If the analogy of a "mega-autobiography" is valid, it can show us something about whether the Genesis narratives are to be taken "literally." If one wrote an autobiography and began with a first-person account of one's own birth, we would have reason to ask whether it is a "literal" account. The description of one's birth would most appropriately be given literally and realistically in an autobiography, but it would nevertheless lie outside the range of what an autobiography is expected to do. We would rather expect one's first recollections of childhood. To write a first-person account of one's own birth would require a virtually impossible kind of author. Thus, in terms of the expectations of an autobiography, the question of whether it is to be taken literally and realistically is not the most important or the most valid question.

The more obvious question would be, How could such an account be called an autobiography? The subject matter itself — one's own birth — would seem to rule out that possibility. That subject matter would lead us to conclude that the birth account was not to be understood in the same way as the rest of the autobiography. It would not lead us to read the birth account any differently; we would read it realistically and literally. The point is that we would not read it from within the same perspective as the rest of the autobiography.

How, then, are we to understand the kind of literature we find in Genesis 1? We can ask if it is to be read "literally," but that is not the most important question. The more important question is whether it is, in fact, a "historical" account.

The categories with which "history" usually deals seem insufficient for the subject of creation. The notion of the Genesis narratives being read literally and realistically is more or less included in the notion of their being history. Simply because the creation narratives are greater than history does not mean they should not be read realistically and literally. It simply means that to understand the literal meaning of Genesis 1, one needs a kind of investigation that contains categories that both include and are greater than everyday experience. To say Genesis 1 is "history" is to limit its meaning to our own historical experience. To say Genesis 1 is "mega-history" means it is to be understood as a realistic and literal depiction of realities that transcend our own historical experiences.

WHEN ANALOGIES FALL SHORT

Let's take an example from the study of history itself. In order to describe the past, historians inevitably use "analogies." An analogy shows how similar events happened in the past and in the present. Historians describe the past by comparing it to events in the present. Understanding history means seeing elements of past events as similar to elements of present events. The past "is like" (analogous to) the present. Such an approach is characteristic of all modern historical research.

In speaking of creation, however, historians are faced with a major problem. "Creation" does not happen every day. It lies at the beginning of our everyday experience but not within it. Thus in approaching the question of the "history" of creation, we need to find analogies between our present, everyday experiences and the unique event of creation. Thinking of the history of creation as a "mega-history" allows us to seek analogies of creation in our everyday experience and, at the same time, to understand them in ways that go beyond those experiences. We can find "analogies" by extending our everyday experiences beyond their everyday applications.

For example, we can see and experience the sunrise at the beginning of each day. The sunrise marks, in a significant way, the beginning of each day in our lives. Using the sunrise as an analogy, it would be appropriate to see the beginning of creation in terms of just such a fundamentally important, daily event. Just as each day of our lives begins with the sunrise, so the beginning of God's six days of creation began with a sunrise. That is, in fact, what the Genesis narrative appears to suggest in Genesis 1:3: "God said, 'Let there be light.'" The sunrise is the act of God with which the author begins his account of the week of creation. On the first day of the week, God causes the sun to rise and dispels the darkness of the night. That initial act is echoed throughout the remainder of the account in the words, "It was evening and it was morning." The days of creation are thus defined and initiated by the arrival of the morning sunlight.

Incidentally, later biblical writers did not miss the importance of that concept for their hope of a future redemption and transformation of God's creation. The image of a sunrise is central to biblical eschatology. The sunrise marks the beginning of the new heavens and the new earth.

SHOULD "DAYS" BE TAKEN LITERALLY?

That leads to another question: Are the "days" in Genesis 1 to be taken literally? That question can be answered in several ways. The "meta-historical" approach to Genesis 1 would say the "days" need not be understood as actual twenty-four-hour days. The sunrise that begins each "day" is merely an image which depicts a real event but does not do so literally. To compare that approach with an autobiography, we could say that a "meta-autobiography" could equally well begin with a sunrise, because a sunrise would be an appropriate image of birth.

A "mega-historical" approach to Genesis 1, on the other hand, would insist that the creation narrative be taken realistically and literally. As such, the narrative is also historical. That means we can understand it by analogies from our own experience.

As mega-history, however, we must understand the biblical narrative to use analogies that ultimately transcend our everyday experience. The "days" of Genesis 1 are thus real and literal twenty-four-hour days, but they depict events that lie outside our everyday experience. That first week was a real and literal week — one like we ourselves experience every seven days — but that first week was not like any other week. God did an extraordinary work in that week, causing its events to transcend by far anything which has occurred since.

If the Genesis account was merely historical in the sense that all other human events are historical, we would have to find actual analogies of creation in our everyday world. If we could do that, creation would not be a unique event and it would, in fact, not be the kind of creation described in Genesis 1 — namely, creation out of nothing. In my opinion, this is precisely what has been done by those who explain creation in terms of the modern notion of the "Big Bang" theory.

According to the "Big Bang" theory, the universe began at some point in the distant past with an immense explosion. A very small and highly dense piece of matter exploded, and the present universe is nothing more than the extended result of that explosion. In effect, we are living in the aftermath of a huge cosmic blast of mass and energy. What we see around us are the fragmentary pieces of that blast. By linking the Genesis creation account with the notion of a primeval cosmic explosion, some interpreters believe they can show the biblical account to be factual, historical, and, therefore, scientific.

In doing so, however, the biblical concept of creation out of nothing loses its meaning. When understood as the "Big Bang," creation becomes just another example of the forces of the physical world we see around us today. Or, to say it another way, the world we see around us is understood merely as a part of the subsequent stages of the "Big Bang." When an astronomer studies the effect of the "Big Bang," he studies only the result of a physical process. When we observe the universe expanding away from itself, we are merely looking at the last part of the explosion.

By identifying God's act of creation with an element or a feature of our own experience of the world, we lose sight of the actual work of God in creation. The biblical account of creation is specifically designed to take us out of our everyday world and to put us back into the world at the time of God's creating it. We thereby come to see our world as a product of God's direct action. The world becomes for us a divine artifact.

Viewed thus as a "mega-history," the biblical account of creation would lead an astronomer to study the universe as God's creation. It shows us that creation is a unique event. In so far as the biblical account in Genesis 1 is able to speak about it in terms understandable to us today, it must do so by means of real analogies. A "real analogy" is a similarity that exists between an everyday event in our world — for example, a sunrise — and an absolutely unique event in the past — for example, a creation.

I maintain that the Genesis narratives are to be understood literally and realistically. They describe real events in literal terms. We can understand them from our own experiences of the world because many of God's acts in creation were analogous to events in our own day. We should not lose sight of the fact, however, that the events of creation were not ordinary events. They were, from a human perspective, unique and unrepeatable acts of God. They were the basis of the existence of the world which we now know and understand through science. Without creation there would not be a world. Our world, however, cannot be traced back to the divine act of creation. Science and history will always be separated from the divine acts of creation. Science and history are always concerned with the world that now exists, while creation is concerned with the existence of the world. "Mega-history" is the notion that God has revealed a history of creation in literal and realistic narratives.

CREATION OUT OF NOTHING

T he most common approach to Genesis 1 today among evangelicals (besides "Scientific Creationism") is to treat Genesis 1:1 as a title. Yet most readers don't realize the problem this creates.

To see Genesis 1:1 as a title actually excludes the theologically essential notion of *creatio ex nihilo*, or "creation out of nothing." In this short chapter I want you to see how my view preserves the traditional sense of Genesis 1:1 as *creatio ex nihilo*. I want to put your mind at ease. You are not giving up anything theologically essential by considering my view — in fact, you will find new support for this critical point.

KEY TO THE CHRISTIAN MESSAGE

One central feature of the traditional interpretation of Genesis 1:1 not only finds solid support in the text but also is of the utmost importance to the Christian message today. That is the belief that God created the universe "out of nothing."

Of course, such a belief flies in the face of modern science, with its dogma of the eternality of the material world. Yet on this point, the Bible cannot be made to say otherwise than that only God is eternal. The material world is a result of His unique plan and purpose.

Though I believe the focus of the first two chapters of Genesis lies on the promised land, I also believe that, before moving to that concern, the biblical writer opens with a view of God and His creation that is nothing short of staggering. He insists that everything that we see around us — the sun, the moon, the stars, the distant galaxies, the seas, the animals, the plants — was created by God. Unlike God, it did not always exist. God is without beginning and without end; the universe is not.

In questioning the concept of *creatio ex nihilo* in Genesis 1:1, a great deal of discussion has centered on the meaning of the Hebrew word translated "created" (*bara*) in Genesis 1:1. The word is used several times in the first chapter (1:21, 27; 2:3–4) but rarely after that (5:1–2; 6:7).

Biblical scholars have traditionally understood the word to mean "to create out of nothing." God did not create the world from some material which already existed. He created the world from "nothing," from "nonexistence." This means that before the world was created, nothing existed but God. Only God existed, and "in the beginning" He created the material universe.

Sometimes the concept of "creation from nothing" is misunderstood to mean that God created the world from some sort of "nothingness" — as if "nothingness" was the source of the material world. That is not what is meant. What is meant by "creation from nothing" is that God started with nothing and merely called the material world into being.

The concept of "creation out of nothing" is an ancient idea. It was already being discussed in the early Hellenistic period (second century B.C.). According to the Apostle Paul, Abraham believed that God called "into existence the things that do not exist" (Romans 4:17), while the author of the Book of Hebrews understood Genesis 1:1 to teach "that the world was created by the word of God, so that what is seen was made out of things which do not appear" (Hebrews 11:3).

As important as these witnesses are to the meaning of Genesis 1:1, we must still raise the question of whether the Hebrew term *bara* actually means "to create out of nothing." And more importantly, is that idea present in the narrative of Genesis 1?

TWO SEPARATE ISSUES

It is now generally recognized that the concept of "creation out of nothing" and the meaning of the word *bara* are two separate issues. Given the nature of biblical narratives such as Genesis 1, it is virtually impossible to prove that the Hebrew word *bara*, by itself, means all that the concept of "creation out of nothing" entails. That would be an enormous concept to be contained in a single word.

What we can say, however, is that the authors of the Hebrew Bible saw in the word *bara* a term which uniquely expressed their understanding of the nature of divine creation. The verb *bara* was used in the Bible only when God was the subject of the action. In the view of the biblical authors, only Israel's God could be said to have "created" (*bara*) anything. Virtually anyone could "make" something (that is the Hebrew word *asah*), but only God could "create" (*bara*) something. Furthermore, when the term *bara* is used in the Bible, there is never any mention of the material from which something is created.[1] Also, the object of what is "created" is always something *new*.[2]

Such features of the word *bara*, in themselves, do not prove that the term can *only* mean "to create out of nothing." Those features do show, however, that *bara* was uniquely suited to express such an idea.

If, as I believe, Genesis 1 intended to teach that God created the world "out of nothing," then the Hebrew word *bara* would not only be well suited for that use, but also would be the only appropriate term that could be chosen. By itself, *bara* would probably not mean all that the concept of "creation from nothing" entails. Within the context of Genesis 1, however, it would have been the most appropriate Hebrew term available.[3]

LARGER CONTEXT

Biblical scholars have long believed the idea of "creation from nothing" can be found in the opening phrase of Genesis 1. I believe there is considerable justification within the text for that view.

When one takes a close look at the opening statement in Genesis 1:1 — particularly in the way it is rendered in most English translations: "In the beginning God created the heavens and the earth" — there is little else the text *could* mean other than "creation out of nothing." The simple notion that the world has a "beginning" would itself seem to necessitate that it was created "from nothing." A "beginning" suggests an origin, a starting point. It suggests that the material world had a starting point and did not always exist. At some time it came into existence.

Those who oppose the idea of "creation out of nothing" being taught in Genesis 1:1 try to support their view by retranslating the verse. The traditional translation — "In the beginning" — implies creation "from nothing." If the translation of Genesis 1:1 is changed to something such as, "When God created the heavens and the earth, the earth was formless and void," the loss of the concept of "creation from nothing" is immediate and transparent.

The doctrine of "creation out of nothing" is thus wrapped up in the question of how the first verse of Genesis is to be translated. Though this is not the place to reproduce the extensive arguments in support of the traditional translation, it can be said that the majority of modern biblical scholars believe that such a translation is the most valid.[4]

The idea of "creation out of nothing" is also suggested in that Genesis 1:1 does not mention a "beginning" for God. Although Genesis 1:1 states clearly that the universe had a "beginning," it does not suggest the same for God. The implication is that God existed "before the beginning" — hence, eternally — and that the material world did not. As the creation account opens, in the first verse, only God exists. Until God "created" the "heavens and earth," there simply were no "heavens and earth."

NOTES

CHAPTER ONE

1. Martin Luther, *The Creation: A Commentary on the First Five Chapters of the Book of Genesis*, trans. Henry Cole (Edinburgh: T & T Clark, 1858), 23.
2. Ibid.
3. Ibid.
4. See chapter 9.
5. See Appendix 2, "Creation out of Nothing," for further discussion on this point.

"Three Major Views, Yea There Are Four"
1. J. P. Moreland, *Christianity and the Nature of Science: A Philosophical Investigation* (Grand Rapids: Baker Book House, 1989), 219.

CHAPTER TWO

1. See pages 44–45 for an explanation of this term.
2. See Appendix 1: "Literal, Figurative, or Something Else?"

"Can Biblical Genealogies Tell Us the Age of the Universe?"
1. Benjamin Breckinridge Warfield, "On the Antiquity and the Unity of the Human Race," *Studies in Theology* (Grand Rapids: Baker Book House, 1981), 244.

CHAPTER THREE

1. *bereshit mamleket* (Jeremiah 28:1)
2. The uses of *reshit* in Genesis 10:10 and 49:3 are not temporal. In any event, they have the same meaning as *reshit* in Genesis 1:1.
3. The Hebrew word *reshonah*, for example, means precisely that. It refers to the "beginning" of a series, the "first" element of a list.
4. Franz Delitzsch, *A New Commentary on Genesis* (Minneapolis: Klock & Klock Christian Publishers, 1978), 76.
5. Otto Procksch, *Die Genesis uebersetzt und erklaert* (Leipzig: Deichertsche Veragsbuchhandlung, 1913), 425.
6. Ernst Boeklen, *Die Verwandtschaft der juedisch-christlichen mit der Parsischen Eschatologie* (Goettingen: Vandenhoeck & Ruprecht, 1902), 136.

CHAPTER FOUR

1. The standard biblical Hebrew lexicon, Koehler and Baumgartner, lists five basic meanings for the term *eretz* in the Old Testament: 1. ground, earth (in the sense of soil); 2. piece of ground; 3. territory, country; 4. the whole of the land, the earth (in a global sense); and 5. the underworld, place of the dead. *The Hebrew & Aramaic Lexicon of the Old Testament*, vol. 1 (Leiden: Brill, 1994), 90–91.
2. For examples, see John H. Sailhamer, *The Pentateuch as Narrative* (Grand Rapids: Zondervan Publishing Co., 1992), 298–99.
3. For example, see Genesis 44:3; Exodus 10:23; Judges 19:26.
4. Yet such an interpretation raises another question. Doesn't Genesis 1 suggest that the sun was created on the fourth day (Genesis 1:14–16)?

Indeed, a straightforward reading of the English text suggests that on the fourth day God created the "sun, moon, and stars." But how could this be so if God created the sun, moon, and stars "in the beginning"? Or to say it another way: If the universe in Genesis 1:1 did not yet include the sun, moon, and stars, then it must have been quite an incomplete "universe." What would the idea of "the universe" mean if it did not include the sun and the stars?

Thus there appears to be an internal contradiction within the Genesis creation account. The events of the fourth day don't seem to square with the clear statement in Genesis 1:1 that God created "everything" in the beginning.

This question has long troubled interpreters of Genesis 1. It has, in fact, often been responsible for setting the agenda for interpreting the rest of the chapter. Classic interpreters solved the problem by supposing that God created a primeval chaos "in the beginning," then from that material carved out the sun and moon and stars on the fourth day. This view dominated the interpretation of Genesis 1 for most of its history.

A better solution lies in the way verses 14 and 16 should be translated. The construction of the Hebrew sentence in verse 14 does not imply that God made the heavenly lights on the fourth day. It does not say, "and God said, 'Let there be lights in the expanse to divide between the day and the night....'" Rather, it says, "And God said, 'Let the lights in the expanse be for dividing between the day and night....'" Do you see the difference? The text does not say God *created* the lights in verse 14, but rather that God *explains why* He created the lights in the expanse — to divide between the day and night, etc.

When, then, did God create the lights? He created them in verse 1 when He created the "heavens and earth." If, as I believe, this is the correct translation of verse 14, then verse 16 does not say God made the sun, moon, and stars on the fourth day. Rather, it summarizes the point of God's words in verses 14 and 15: "So God made the two great lights...to rule the day...and to rule the night...."

As I understand it, the proper translation of Genesis 1:14–17 is as follows:

[14] And God said, "Let the lights in the expanse of the sky be for dividing between day and night and for signs, seasons, days, and years and [15] let them be for light sources in the expanse of the sky to provide light for the land." Now that was precisely what came about. [16] So we see that God made the two big lights (the larger to rule the day and the lesser to rule the night) and the stars and [17] he put them in the expanse of the sky to give light to the land.

For further explanation of this interpretation, see the *Expositor's Bible Commentary* (Grand Rapids: Zondervan Publishing Co., 1990), on this verse.

CHAPTER FIVE

1. "informis et inanis," cf. *Calvin's Commentary*. Calvin's comments on these words show that his understanding of the translation "unformed and empty" was already beginning to shift away from the Greek concept of chaos and toward a more biblical notion of "uninhabitable land." It was, as well, quite different from the image his own translation ("unformed and empty") may suggest to the modern reader.

2. John Calvin, *Commentaries on the First Book of Moses Called Genesis*, trans. John King (Grand Rapids: Baker Book House, 1979), 73. Yet for Calvin, the "shapeless chaos" was not a cosmic gas cloud or an unformed chaos but a stretch of land devoid of all those features added to it by God during the six days of Genesis 1.

3. *The New Scofield Bible* (New York: Oxford University Press, 1967).

4. Hugh Ross, *Genesis One: A Scientific Perspective* (Sierra Madre: Wisemen Publications, 1983), 5–6.

5. The meaning of the word *tohu* ("formless") is identical to that of Isaiah 45:18: "[God] did not create it [the land] to be empty [*tohu*], but formed it to be inhabited." The term "empty" (*tohu*) in the Isaiah passage stands in opposition to the phrase "to be inhabited." This is the same meaning of *tohu* found in Deuteronomy 32:10. There, "formless" (*tohu*) is parallel to "desert" (*midbar*), an uninhabitable wasteland.

CHAPTER SIX

1. It is still unclear how the reference to "east" in 2:8, which seems positive, is to be associated with the references to "eastward" in the subsequent narratives, which are all to be taken negatively. One solution may be that of the early versions. The Targum of Onkelos, for example, translated it as "long ago" rather than as "eastward" (cf. the Vulgate's *a principio*). Both meanings are possible for the Hebrew expression. In any event, if a geographical direction is meant here, the author is apparently establishing an important dis-

tinction between "east" and "west," which will be of great thematic importance throughout the remainder of the book.

2. For examples of the historical search for the garden of Eden, see chapter 23.

3. Interestingly, the amount of description for each of the four rivers is in inverse proportion to the certainty of its identification. Although the narrative pays most attention to the Pishon, there is least certainty regarding its identification and location. On the other hand, the narrative merely states that the well-known River Euphrates is the fourth river.

4. cf. Ezekiel 36:35 — "This land that was laid waste has become like the garden of Eden"; Joel 2:3 — "Before them the land is like the garden of Eden, behind them, a desert waste"; Isaiah 51:3 — "The LORD will surely comfort Zion and will look with compassion on all her ruins; he will make her deserts like Eden, her wastelands like the garden of the LORD"; Zechariah 14:8 — "On that day living water will flow out from Jerusalem"; Revelation 22:1–2 — "Then the angel showed me the river of the water of life, as clear as crystal, flowing from the throne of God and of the Lamb down the middle of the great street of the city. On each side of the river stood the tree of life, bearing twelve crops of fruit, yielding its fruit every month."

5. This relationship has also been discussed by Gordon J. Wenham, "Sanctuary Symbolism in the Garden of Eden Story," *Proceedings of the World Congress of Jewish Studies*, 9 (1986), 19–25.

6. The difference between the spelling of "to work it" and "to worship" is slight. See the explanation in the *Expositor's Bible Commentary,* vol 2, p. 47.

CHAPTER SEVEN

1. *Religion in Geschichte und Gegenwart*, (RGG), vol. 6 (Tuebingen: J. C. B. Mohr (Paul Siebeck), 1957), 1611.

2. James B. Pritchard, *Ancient Near East Texts* (Princeton: Princeton University Press, 1969), 67–68.

3. John H. Walton, *Ancient Israelite Literature in Its Cultural Context* (Grand Rapids: Zondervan Publishing Co., 1989), 34–38.

CHAPTER EIGHT

1. For a comprehensive discussion of the author's views on the nature and purpose of the Pentateuch, see Sailhamer, *The Pentateuch As Narrative.*

CHAPTER NINE

1. Judging from the author's style in Genesis, summary statements at the beginning of a narrative are, as a rule, nominal clauses (e.g. Genesis 2:4a; 5:1; 6:9; 11:10). When verbal clauses serve as summaries, they are attached to the end of the narrative (e.g., Genesis 2:1; 25:34b; 49:28b). Francis I. Andersen, *The Sentence in Biblical Hebrew* (The Hague: Mouton Publishers, 1974), 53.

2. The conjunction "and" (Hebrew: *waw*) at the beginning of 1:2 shows that 1:2–2:4 is coordinated with 1:1, rather than appositional. If the first verse were intended as a summary of the rest of the chapter, it would be appositional and hence would not be followed by the conjunction, e.g., Genesis 2:4a; 5:1. The conjunction in Genesis 2:5a further demonstrates the role of the conjunction in coordinating clauses, e.g., (2:4b) "When the LORD God made earth and heaven, (2:5) now [Hebrew conjunction *waw*] there was not yet any shrub of the field...(2:7) the LORD God made man...."

3. See particularly Gordon Wenham's observations in the *Word Biblical Commentary,* vol. 1 (Waco: Word Books, 1987), 6, as well as Sailhamer, *The Pentateuch As Narrative, passim.*

CHAPTER TEN

1. The Hebrew text reads "one day" rather than "first day." See *Expositor's Bible Commentary,* vol. 2, p. 28 for a further discussion of the meaning of this expression.

CHAPTER ELEVEN

1. Delitzsch, *Commentary on Genesis*, 86.
2. Calvin, *First Book of Moses*, 80. "Moreover, the word *rq'* comprehends not only the whole region of the air, but whatever is open above us: as the word heaven is sometimes understood by the Latins."
3. Ibid.
4. Ibid. "For, to my mind, this is a certain principle, that nothing is here treated of but the visible form of the world. He who would learn astronomy, and other recondite arts, let him go elsewhere."
5. Hermann Gunkel, for example, lists many examples of the ancient conceptualization of the world as enclosed by a global "vaulted ceiling." *Genesis uebersetzt und erklaert* (Goettingen: Vandenhoeck & Ruprecht, 1977), 107.
6. Claus Westermann, *Biblischer Kommentar Altes Testament: Genesis* (Neukirchen-Vluyn: Neukirchener Verlag, 1983), 116.
7. Henry Morris, *Scientific Creationism* (El Cajon: Master Books, 1985), 210–11.
8. Westermann, *Genesis*, 113–23.
9. That, incidentally, is how the psalmist read this text. He tells us simply that "God spoke, and it came to pass" (Psalm 33:9).
10. Robert de Beaugrade and Wolfgang Dressler, *Introduction to Text Linguistics* (London: Longman, 1981), 163ff.

CHAPTER TWELVE

1. For example, the bronze basin made for temple worship is also called a "sea" (see 1 Kings 7:23–25, 39, 44).

CHAPTER THIRTEEN

1. C. F. Keil and F. Delitzsch, *Biblical Commentary on the Old Testament* (Grand Rapids: Wm. B. Eerdmans Publishing Co., 1971), 59.
2. Calvin, *First Book of Moses*, 70.
3. M. Rosenbaum and A. M. Silbermann, trans., *Pentateuch with Tagum Onkelos, Haphtaroth and Prayers for Sabbath and Rashi's Commentary, Genesis* (London: Shapiro, Vallentine and Co., 1929), 5.
4. Scofield, *New Scofield Reference Bible*, 1. Cf. Zoeckler, "Schoepfung," *Real-Encyklopaidie fuer protestanitische Theologie und Kirche*, XX, 1866, 735f.
5. Ross, *Genesis One*, 10.
6. In chapter 9 we considered the difficulties with understanding Genesis 1:1 as a title for the whole chapter. I believe it is virtually impossible to read it that way in the Hebrew text. Many well-qualified biblical scholars, however, have accepted the notion that Genesis 1:1 is a title. For that reason we cannot dismiss it out of hand.
7. H. H. Schmid, *Theologisches Handwoerterbuch zum Alten Testament*, Band I, 1971, 229.
8. It is for that reason that the Hebrew word for "lights" (*'or*) grammatically does not have the article, "the" lights. It would not have been proper Hebrew for the article to have been used until the "lights" had been specifically referred to in the previous narrative.
9. The Hebrew verb *hyh* alone.
10. The Hebrew verb *hyh* with an infinitive; cf. Emil Kautsch and A. E. Cowley, *Gesenius' Hebrew Grammar* (Oxford: The Clarendon Press, 1910), 348h.

CHAPTER FOURTEEN

1. See *Expositor's Bible Commentary*, vol. 2, p. 35, for a discussion of the use of the term *bara* in the creation account.
2. The specific animals that filled the land at God's command on the fifth day would not, of course, be the same individual animals created "in the beginning." As I have understood it, the time period of "the beginning" could have been eons of years. Many species of animal life could have come into being and then fallen into extinction during that time. The creatures which God commands to fill the waters and skies of "the land" would have

been those which were flourishing at the time. The narrative picture given in Genesis 1 is thus similar to the animals which came to the ark at the time of the flood.

CHAPTER FIFTEEN

1. Westermann, *Genesis*, 144f; Eduard Koenig, *Die Genesis eingeleitet, uebersetzt und erklaert*, (Guetersloh: C. Bertelsmann, 1925), 153.
2. Westermann, *Genesis*, 144f.
3. Karl Barth, *Church Dogmatics*, III/1, (Edinburgh: T & T Clark, 1958), 195.
4. Claus Westermann, *Theologie des Alten Testaments in Grundzuegen*, (Goettingen: Vandenhoeck & Ruprecht, 1978), 75.

"The Age of Humankind"

1. Marlise Simons, "French Scientists Date the Oldest Cave," *The New York Times*, 8 June 1995.
2. John Noble Wilford, "Genetic Sleuths Follow Clues to Elusive Ancestral 'Adam,'" *The New York Times*, 23 November 1995, A1.

CHAPTER SIXTEEN

1. See *Expositor's Bible Commentary*.
2. Ibid.

CHAPTER SEVENTEEN

"Is Life Extra-Terrestrial?"

1. James Trefil, "However it began on Earth, life may have been inevitable," originally published in *Smithsonian Magazine*, February 1995, 13.

CHAPTER EIGHTEEN

1. John Lightfoote, *A few and new observations upon the book of Genesis. The most of them certain, the rest probable, all harmless, strange, and rarely heard of before* (London: T. Badger, 1642).

CHAPTER NINETEEN

1. It can hardly be doubted that the Bible's view of creation is geocentric; it clearly focuses on earthly events. Yet that does not imply that it sees the earth as the center of the universe. The biblical account merely tells the story of creation from the perspective of a person living on the earth. The account would be quite different had it been written by a Martian. But since the focus of the Genesis account is on the earth, therefore, the sun, moon, and stars are all viewed from that perspective.
2. Ross, *Genesis One*, 1.
3. The Wisdom of Solomon 11:17, "For thine all-powerful hand, That created the world out of formless matter [*ek amorphou uleis*]" Charles, ed., *The Apocrypha and Pseudepigrapha*, 553.
4. Ibid.
5. "By faith we understand that the world was created by the word of God, so that what is seen was not made out of what was visible" (Hebrews 11:3).
6. John 1:3.

CHAPTER TWENTY

1. Scholder, *Urspruenge und Probleme der Bibelkritik*, 57.
2. Ibid., 56–78.
3. Peter Batholinus (Lutheran, 1632); Gisbert Voeet (Reformed, 1634). See, Scholder, 66. Otto Zoeckler, *Geschichte der Beziehungen zwischen Theologie und Naturwissenschaft mit besondrer Rueckcsicht auf Schoepfungsgeschichte* (Guetersloh: C. Bertelsmann, 1877), 72.

4. For example, Flood Geology, the Gap Theory, the Day-Age Theory, and the Mythological interpretation of Genesis 1 and 2.

5. Zoeckler, *Geschichte der Beziehungen*, 72.

CHAPTER TWENTY-ONE

1. "Coelum et terram vocat, non qualia nunc sunt, sed rudia adhuc et informia corpora." Martin Luther, *In Primum Librum Mose Enarrationes, Exegetica Opera Latina*, vol. 1, ed. C. S. T. Elsperger (Erlangen: Carl Heyder, 1829), 11.

2. "Simpliciter enim hoc voluit Moses, non statim ab initio sed inane caeli et terrae chaos fuisse creatum." *Opera Omnia*, Amsterdam, 1671, 2.

3. *The Bible, That is, The holy Scriptures conteined in the Olde and Newe Testament*, London, 1599.

4. J. I. Mombert, ed., *William Tyndale's Five Books of Moses Called the Pentateuch*, (Carbondale: Southern Illinois University Press, 1967).

5. "terra autem erat inanis et vacua…" Robert Weber, ed., *Biblia Sacra Iuxta Vulgatam Versionem* (Stuttgart: Deutsche Bibelgesellschaft, 1983).

6. See Codex Neofiti 1 on Genesis 1:1 and the book of Jubilees 7:1.

7. *Ibn Ezra's Commentary on the Pentateuch, Genesis (Bereshit)*, (New York: Menorah Publishing Co., 1988), 29–30.

8. Silbermann, 5.

9. Keil and Delitzsch, *Biblical Commentary*, 59.

10. This was the view of Paul Fagius, *Critica Sacra*, 6; and Ramban.

"The Origin of Life"
1. Trefil, "However it began," 2.

CHAPTER TWENTY-TWO

1. In the earliest expositions of Genesis 1 it was plainly and routinely stated that the first verse described God's creation of an "unformed mass" of matter which He later shaped into the present world. Among the early commentators on Genesis who expressly state this view are Augustine (*Lib. I. De Genesis contra Manichaeos*, cap. vii); Luther (*In Primum Librum Mose Enarrationes*, Erlangen, 1829, p. 11); Calvin (*Commentaries on the First Book of Moses called Genesis*, Baker, 1979, p. 70); and Cornelius a Lapide (*Commentaria in Scripturam Sacram*, Paris, 1868, vol. i, p. 44).

2. D. Martini Lutheri, *Exegetica Opera Latina*, vol. 1, C. S. R. Elsperger, ed., Erlangen, 1829, p. 26.

3. "an ista lux se moverit motu circulari?" Ibid.

4. "Ego quidem fateor me verum nescire; si quis tamen scire cupiat, quid mihi simillimum veri vidatur, existimo istam lucem fuisse mobilem, ita ut lux illa fecerit naturalem diem, ab ortum in occasum." Ibid.

5. Ibid.

6. "Moses enim diserte dicit, fuisse lucem, et numerat hunc primum diem creationis." Ibid.

7. "Ergo Dominus ipso creationis ordine, lucem se in manu habere testatur: quam nobis largiri possit absque sole et luna." Ibid., 3.

8. Rosenbaum and Silbermann, *Rashi's Commentary*, 5.

9. Lutheri, *Exegetica Opera Latina*, 51.

10. "Nihil enim aliud refert Moses quam Deum certa organa destinasse quae lucem jam prius creatam, mutuis vicibus per mundum diffunderent." Ibid., 4.

11. "Hoc tantum est discrimen, quod prius erat lux sparsa, nunc a corporibus lucidis procedit…." Ibid.

12. *Realencyklopaedie fuer protestantische Theologie und Kirche*, 3d ed. vol. 17 (Leipzig: J. C. Hinrichs'sche Verlag, 1896), 695.

13. Ibid.

14. Jerusalem, 1768; Doederlein, 1780.

15. G. Andre de Luc, 1779; George Cuvier, 1812.

16. Zoeckler, *Geschichte der Beziehungen*, 499–500.

CHAPTER TWENTY-THREE

1. We should keep in mind that at the time this understanding of the term "earth" was taking root in the Church, very little was actually known of the scope or extent of the "earth" outside the limits of the Roman Empire and the regions which bordered it.

2. Chaim D. Shual, *Rashi's Commentary on the Torah* (Jerusalem: Harav Kook Publishers, 1988), 1.

3. John Lightfoote, *A Few, and New Observations, upon the Booke of Genesis* (London: T. Badger, 1642), 2.

4. See John Pye Smith, *On the Relation Between the Holy Scriptures and some Parts of Geological Science* (New York: D. Appleton and Co., 1840), 232–33.

5. *Real-Encyklopaedie fuer protestantische Theologie und Kirche,* 1st ed. vol. 20 (Gotha: Rudolf Besser, 1866), 334.

6. Ibid.

7. Ibid., 338.

8. *Notae ad Sansonis Geographiam sacram. Ugolini Thesaurus biblicus.* also: *Commentar zur Genesis,* 1699.

9. *Real-Encyklopaedie,* 339.

10. De situ Paradisi terrestris, *Opera selecta,* 1709.

11. *Dissertatio de situ Paradisi terrestris, Dissertationum miscell.* partes tres, 1706–1708.

12. Calvin, *First Book of Moses,* 113.

APPENDIX I

1. Hermann Gunkel, *Genesis uebersetzt und erklaert* (Goettingen: Vandenhoeck & Ruprecht, 1977), 117.

2. An excellent discussion of the view of history represented here is found in John Goldingay, *Models for Scripture* (Grand Rapids: Eerdmanns Publishing Co., 1994), 39–60.

3. V. Philips Long's recent insights on the parable of Lazarus and the rich man in Luke 16 are helpful on this point. See V. Philips Long, *The Art of Biblical History* (Grand Rapids: Zondervan, 1994), 41–42.

APPENDIX 2

1. That does not necessarily mean that there was no material. It simply means that the material, if there was such, is not envisioned in the word *bara.*

2. Ernst Jenni and Claus Westermann, eds., *Theologisches Handwoerterbuch zum Alten Testament,* vol. 1 (Muenchen: Chr. Kaiser Verlag, 1971), 337–38.

3. We must be careful to distinguish between individual words and the concepts they help express. In any language, the concept a word may help express is almost always larger than any single word. Concepts arise out of the meaning of texts more than out of the meaning of individual words. Words are not mere labels for concepts. Words are the building blocks of mental images and concepts. Thus we must look beyond the Hebrew word *bara* itself for an understanding of the concept of "creation out of nothing" in Genesis 1:1.

4. See arguments in "Genesis," *Expoositor's Bible Commentary,* vol. 2, 21.